Road Cycling in Central Virginia

A Guide

Sue George

UNIVERSITY OF VIRGINIA PRESS CHARLOTTESVILLE AND LONDON

University of Virginia Press

Printed in the United States of America on acid-free paper
First published 2006

9 8 7 6 5 4 3 2 1

Library of Congress Cataloging-in-Publication Data
George, Sue, 1975–
Road cycling in central Virginia : a guide / Sue George.
p. cm.
Includes bibliographical references.
ISBN 0-8139-2532-0 (pbk. : alk. paper)
1. Cycling—Virginia—Guidebooks. 2. Virginia—Guidebooks. I. Title.
GV1045.5.V8G46 2006
917.5504'44—dc22 2006004629

This book is dedicated to my parents, Ron and Eileen George. As I was growing up, they encouraged in me a love of cycling as a sport and as a lifestyle. Without it, this book would never have existed.

Contents

Acknowledgments

I would like to thank my husband, Matthew Wikswo, for his enduring support and patience while I spent two years researching and preparing this book. Having lived in central Virginia for more than a dozen years, and as a regular user of guidebooks for cycling, hiking, and climbing, Matthew was an excellent adviser regarding many aspects of this book. I also appreciated his company while scouting some of the routes.

The expertise of the following local cyclists contributed greatly to this book as they led me on rides all over central Virginia. Thank you for showing me the many great cycling roads in your home areas: Thomas Jenkins (Rockingham County), Marcia Lamphier (Rockingham County, Augusta County), Marshall Hammond (Rockingham County, Augusta County), Peter O'Shaughnessy (Augusta County), John Whitaker (Albemarle County, Augusta County), and Char St. Laurent (Albemarle County).

While I explored and re-explored these areas, I often enjoyed the company of one or more of my favorite riding buddies. I cannot list everyone with whom I rode while researching this book, but special thanks go to Michael Smoot, David Wotton, and Jon Thornburg. These individuals and many others provided general encouragement along the way, and were forgiving even when I had to miss epic mountain bike rides to go exploring on my road bike!

And finally, thank you to my editor, Boyd Zenner, who suggested and encouraged this guidebook and who was patient with me while I simultaneously tried to be a wife, race my mountain bike, pursue mountain bike advocacy work, write freelance articles, and run a local bike club, all while working full-time as a project manager and researching and writing this book.

Introduction

Since moving from Pennsylvania to the Charlottesville area in 1997, I have ridden all over the rolling Piedmont, in the Blue Ridge Mountains, and in the Shenandoah Valley. The pleasant roads, beautiful scenery, and mild climate have brought me countless enjoyable hours on the bike, solo and with companions.

I'm often asked by inexperienced riders or those new to the area, "Where should I ride?" This book gives the answer.

I geared the book toward beginner and intermediate recreational riders who are looking for road cycling routes. I have deliberately stayed away from passes climbing over the Blue Ridge Mountains or into the Alleghenies. I've also omitted gravel roads as well as paved roads with high traffic volume, as many beginner and intermediate riders find these intimidating. That means not every favorite local road has made it into this book.

Most rides are between 15 and 30 miles in length, with a few shorter or longer. There are almost no flat roads in this region, so riders who struggle on hills will want to pick shorter routes to compensate for the rolling, sometimes steep local terrain. Or they may prefer to do out-and-back rides on portions of the routes, while gradually building up more fitness and skill.

Since all the routes finish at the place they start, any climbing is rewarded with an equal amount of downhill. In fact, the numerous hills of the region provide cyclists with many good views of the Blue Ridge and Allegheny Mountains. Without these, the scenery, and thus the riding experience, would be much less interesting.

More experienced riders or racers also will enjoy this book, particularly if they are not familiar with the area. New residents and tourists will quickly get a good sense of the best areas in which to ride after completing several routes. They can then link various rides together or use local maps to create longer routes, exploring on their own as they feel comfortable. Also, because there are many hills in the area, riders who wish for a tougher workout can simply push harder on the climbs to challenge themselves if they don't have the inclination to ride longer distances.

Starting and finishing points for the rides are always public places, such as town parks or schools.

The rolling green woodlands and farmlands of the Shenandoah Valley and the western Piedmont constitute one of my favorite road riding areas in the United States. I hope it will become one of your favorites as well.

How do I use this book?

This book covers rides leaving from and venturing into the following localities: the cities of Charlottesville (and surrounding towns), Harrisonburg, Waynesboro, Bridgewater, Dayton, Grottoes, Stanardsville, and Staunton, and the counties of Albemarle, Greene, Augusta, and Rockingham.

The book is divided into two parts. The introduction provides general information for cyclists riding in this area. The second part contains descriptions of routes suitable for beginner, intermediate, and expert riders. Each ride has a cue sheet, map, and basic information. Rides are listed by geographic area based on starting location, so you can pick your region and then pick your ride within that region. (Note: Some rides cross regions as defined in this book. For example, the Grottoes ride starts in Rockingham County, but because Grottoes is located on the county line, nearly all of the ride occurs in Augusta County.)

For each ride, the following information is provided:

RIDE NAME Most names include the town where the ride originates and finishes. When a town hosts more than one ride, directional information is also provided. For example, the Charlottesville Northwest ride starts from Charlottesville and heads generally northwest. Other towns through which the route passes also are listed.

SUMMARY The summary provides an overview of the route. For example, it may mention that the route is particularly well shaded or passes by points of interest such as vineyards or caverns.

DISTANCE All routes were clocked with the same odometer. You may find that your odometer reads higher or lower due to inaccuracies in one or both of our measuring tools. In that case, howcvcr, you should read consistently higher or lower mileages for all rides.

ELEVATION CHANGE All elevations were estimated using the National Geographic Back Roads Explorer software (calculations done at level 4) and probably are not exactly what you would measure with a GPS or altimeter. However, the comparisons of elevations between rides are useful in quantifying how relatively flat or hilly a particular route is.

TRAFFIC LEVEL This section estimates the level of traffic (in the author's opinion) and notes stretches of roads that are particularly likely to have more or less traffic. Use caution on all roads, but especially on main roads that may carry more frequent or higher-speed traffic. These include routes with two-digit numbers like Route 42 or Route 29, and routes with three-digit numbers starting with the numeral 2, like Route 257 or Route 250. Traffic level is subjective and likely to change with increasing development over time or at rush hours.

TERRAIN Most rides are hilly due to the local geography, but it is noted if the route is unusually hilly or flat.

STORES ALONG THE ROUTE Riders should never assume stores will be open, and should carry enough food and water to be self-sufficient for the duration of the ride.

START LOCATION All rides finish at the same point at which they started. Directions are given from larger towns or cities and follow major regional roads or U.S. highways, which may not be appropriate for non-motorized travel.

COMMENTS Special notes pertaining to the ride may include comments on sight-seeing possibilities along the way or options for extending or shortening the ride.

DIRECTIONS This section contains an intersection-by-intersection description of the route. Mileage is denoted at each intersection of interest, as are state and local route numbers and local street names. Note that in Virginia, numbers and names are subject to change separately or simultaneously at every intersection. Many intersection points listed require the rider to do nothing but continue straight, but changes in route name or number are noted. This practice was adopted to facilitate riders' completing the routes in reverse if desired. Note that each major intersection is denoted with a letter, which is shown on the corresponding map. If riders encounter an intersection that is not mentioned, they should proceed straight on the road of the same name and route number, following it in its default direction (which may in reality turn obviously left or right).

What's the weather like in central Virginia?

Most years, beginner and intermediate riders will be able to ride spring, summer, and fall with little or no gear beyond shorts, a jersey or T-shirt, and summer-weight gloves. Some years, mild winters facilitate pleasant cycling year-round, and temperatures have been known to regularly hit 60 and 70 degrees Fahrenheit in December and January. Other times, snow and ice limit winter riding and keep high temperatures in the 30s and 40s.

Summers typically are hot and humid (highs in the 80s and 90s). Riders will want to use sunscreen and limit sun exposure and opportunities for dehydration or overheating during the hottest times of the day. They also will need to carry significantly more water in summer months. Severe afternoon thunderstorms are common in the area May through August, but you often can find a picnic shelter or porch roof for cover at short notice.

For many riders, spring and fall are the best times of year to ride due to the moderate temperatures (60s and 70s) and natural beauty. Mild Virginia winters enable a long, slow spring with blooming flowers, shrubs, and trees taking their turns by type from late February through May. The pink, purple, and white flowering redbud, dogwood, cherry, and pear trees are eye candy, and the green of spring can be seen progressing steadily up into the mountains day by day. Similarly, autumn brings color to the area, which is largely covered by deciduous forests. Riders can watch leaves colorfully changing first along the ridge tops and then at lower elevations. The peak of leaf season typically is in late October. Except in winter, something is always in bloom.

What should I take with me?

Cycling is an inherently dangerous and complicated sport, and riders should carry several items with them at all times to be prepared for mechanical failure or a crash. The following items are recommended, but by no means is the list all-inclusive. If you are not mechanically inclined, consider asking your local bike shop or bike club for information or about classes covering basic repairs before you hit the road:

Helmet (wear it at all times!)
Gloves
Glasses
Spare tube(s)
Portable frame or pocket tire pump
Tire levers (for removing the tire to change a flat)
Phillips and flathead screwdrivers
Set of allen keys (sizes 3, 4, and 5 at a minimum)
Chain tool and spare chain link or pin
Adjustable wrench (especially if your wheels are not attached by quick-release mechanism)
Cell phone (note: although coverage is improving, cell phones will not work in many remote areas visited by these rides)
Personal identification such as driver's license or passport
Emergency contact information
Insurance card
Spare layer, such as a jacket or vest
Ride directions and appropriate maps

Before departing on any ride, it is a good idea to tell someone where you are going so they can send help if you do not return within a reasonable amount of time.

How are the roads marked in central Virginia?

In this book, you will find references to U.S. routes, state routes, county routes, and city streets. Virginia localities are divided into counties and cities (cities are not considered part of counties), and most roads featured here are county or city roads.

Virginia public county roads are well marked, usually with a street sign (green, with street name in white), a route number sign (black square with white circle featuring route number in black), or both at every intersection. City streets usually are marked only with a traditional street sign (usually green, blue, or brown with white letters). In rare instances, you will find signs missing, but the mileage cues in this book will help guide you at those turns.

What are the hazards of cycling in central Virginia?

Road cycling is liberating because you can cover so much ground under your own power and take in lots of scenery along the way. However, riders must always be on the defensive and alert for potential hazards.

As with riding anywhere in the United States, cars are probably the greatest hazard. Many drivers don't "see" cyclists, or they try to pass on blind corners or hills with no or low visibility. Many roads in central Virginia are hilly and twisty, so riders need to watch for this behavior and be prepared to react appropriately. Cars are the greatest hazard around rush hours, when drivers are in a hurry to get to or from work. Saturday mornings also can be busy as drivers run errands and take kids to and from sports practices. In general, the rides in this book target lower-traffic roads, but they may include unavoidable short sections on busier roads. The routes avoid most major through roads, but many still must be crossed. Additionally, as more rural lands are subdivided for homes, riders can expect to see traffic levels increasing farther and farther from city or town limits.

Roads in central Virginia tend to have little or no shoulder, and bike lanes are few and far between. Riders should stay as far to the right as practicable, but be aware that many roads have significant drop-offs from the edge of the pavement to the grassy roadside. Therefore, riders should leave enough room to maneuver without riding off the road, particularly if grass and wildflowers are obscuring the view of the edge.

Central Virginia road surfaces generally are maintained in very good condition. If you are used to riding in northern states like Pennsylvania, you will find yourself wondering, "Where are all the potholes and cracks?" Still, be vigilant for unexpected breaks in the pavement, especially during the spring thaw period. The winter freeze/thaw cycle wreaks havoc on paved surfaces.

Central Virginia has many wooden bridges with surfaces of planks running perpendicular to the direction of travel. Each plank has round metal bolt heads in rows to secure it. Use caution on these bridges. They often are narrower than the rest of the road, and the planks and bolt heads can become slippery when wet or after long humid periods. Always brake before you get to the bridges, and ride straight and don't try to brake or turn while crossing them. Because the bridges cross streams, many are at the bottom of fast descents and around blind corners, and you may have to yield to oncoming traffic if the bridge is narrow.

Riders also will encounter railroad tracks. In general, cross them perpendicularly, changing in advance the angle of your direction of travel relative to the road's if necessary. Do not brake, stand up, turn, or accelerate while crossing tracks as they may be slippery, especially when wet.

Animals are a hazard you will regularly encounter in central Virginia. It is not uncommon to see turtles and snakes in the road or rabbits, groundhogs, and squirrels dashing across a street. Deer are everywhere in this region—and I have known a few riders to hit them—so keep an eye out for them on roadsides and be prepared for them to jump out unexpectedly in front of you. Slow when you see any wild animal on or near the road, but don't react suddenly unless warranted. Most will move on their own, given time, and slowing down reduces your risk of crashing or swerving into traffic or the path of other riders.

Dogs may be man's best friend, but they can be a cyclist's worst enemy when they run into the road. Relative to other regions, central Virginia does not have many untied dogs, but ride long enough and you will inevitably encounter some. Here are tips:

- Don't panic. The dog may be friendly and just coming to greet you.
- Look for indications of an invisible fence. It may be marked with flags, or the dog may slow as it nears an obvious property boundary. Many homeowners in the area have installed such fences.
- Talk to the dog in a calm, cheerful voice. Let it know you are harmless. If you shout at it, you may make it more excited or scared, and if it's determined to come your way it will do so no matter how you talk to it. If the dog is used to being mistreated, your shouts may trigger a defensive response. If it is well treated, it will have good associations with a friendly voice.
- Slow down to increase your ability to react if a dog runs in front of you. If the dog seems relentlessly aggressive, you can stop and put your bike between you and it while you wait for it to calm down or for the owner to call it. However, if the dog is particularly mean and you feel confident you can outrun it, sprinting away may be a more attractive option.

What about stores?

Each ride notes country convenience stores (some with gas stations) where riders may restock with water, Gatorade, juice, soda, or food. Small country stores often change owners, go out of business, or close on Sundays or on weekdays and Saturday evenings, so always pack enough food and water for the ride just in case. These country stores seem to be less common in central Virginia than they used to be.

Table of Rides

The following table summarizes all the rides in this guidebook and key characteristics of each for easy reference.

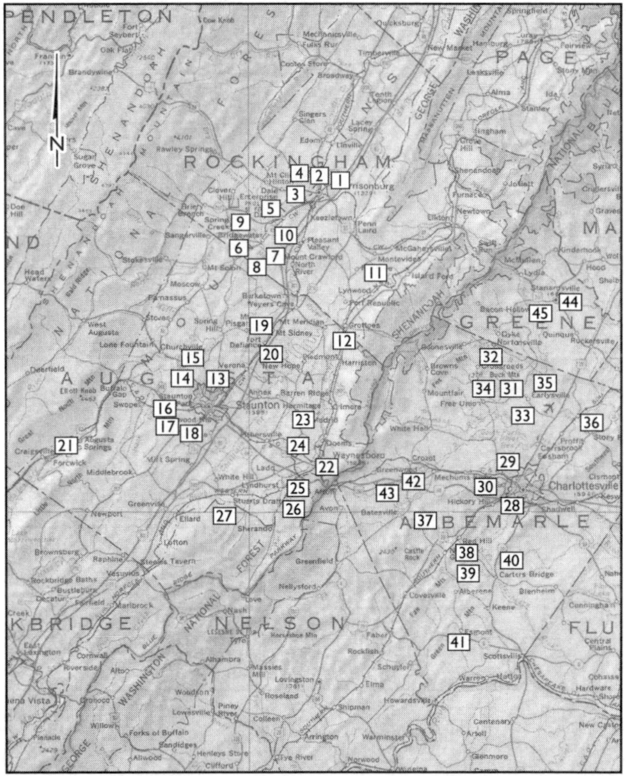

CENTRAL VIRGINIA

RIDE NO.	RIDE NAME	REGION	START LOCATION	DISTANCE (MILES)	OPTIONS (MILES)	ELEVATION (FEET)	PAGE
	Rockingham County Harrisonburg						
1	Harrisonburg Northeast —Keezletown, Zenda	Central Rockingham	Harrisonburg Hillandale Park	31.5	18	1,620	19
2	Harrisonburg North— Zenda, Hightown, Linville, Edom, Green Mount	Central Rockingham	Harrisonburg Hillandale Park	31.5	—	1,735	22
3	Harrisonburg West— Dayton, Rushville, Clover Hill, Lilly, Mt Clinton	Southwest Rockingham	Harrisonburg Hillandale Park	25.0	—	1,500	25
4	Harrisonburg Northwest —Green Mount, Singers Glen, Sparkling Springs, Stultz Mill, Mt Clinton	West Rockingham	Harrisonburg Hillandale Park	35.5	18	1,920	28
	Bridgewater and Dayton						
5	Dayton—Rushville, Hinton, Mole Hill	Southwest Rockingham	Dayton Cooks Creek Park	12.5	—	745	32

6	Bridgewater Southwest—Spring Creek, Sangerville, Stokesville, Mt Solon, Mossy Creek, Centerville	Southwest Rockingham	Bridgewater Wildwood Park	28.4	—	1,060	35
7	Bridgewater Southeast—Airport, Burketown, North River	Augusta/Rockingham line	Bridgewater Wildwood Park	27.0	—	1,150	38
8	Bridgewater South—Airport, Centerville	Augusta/Rockingham line	Bridgewater Wildwood Park	13.5	—	515	41
9	Bridgewater Northwest—Clover Hill, Union Springs, Briery Branch, Spring Creek, Montezuma	Southwest Rockingham	Bridgewater Wildwood Park	24.8	—	750	44
10	Bridgewater East—North River, Cross Keys, Pleasant Valley	South Central Rockingham	Bridgewater Wildwood Park	24.9	—	930	47
	Montevideo						
11	Montevideo—Pineville, Port Republic, Grottoes, Goods Mill	Southeast Rockingham	Montevideo Middle School	23.6	12	680	51

RIDE NO.	RIDE NAME	REGION	START LOCATION	DISTANCE (MILES)	OPTIONS (MILES)	ELEVATION (FEET)	PAGE
	Grottoes						
12	Grottoes—Harriston, Piedmont, Mt Meridian	Northeast Augusta	Grottoes Town Park	16.9	13.7	470	55
	Augusta County Staunton						
13	Staunton Northeast—Quicks Mill, Mt Pisgah, Roman, Spring Hill	North Augusta	Staunton Gypsy Hill Park	25.7	19.5	1,860	61
14	Staunton North (short)—Franks Mill, Spring Hill	Northwest Augusta	Staunton Gypsy Hill Park	19.6	—	1,210	64
15	Staunton North (long)—Spring Hill, Moscow, Mt Solon, Parnassus, Franks Mill	Northwest Augusta	Staunton Gypsy Hill Park	34.6	—	2,580	67
16	Staunton West—Cedar Green, Swoope, Trimbles Mill, Hebron	West Augusta	Staunton Beverley Manor Elementary School	20.9	15	1,325	70

17	Staunton Southwest—Cedar Green, Hebron, Arbor Hill, Middlebrook, Trimbles Mill	Southwest Augusta	Staunton Beverley Manor Elementary School	25.1	—	1,385	73
18	Staunton South—Cedar Green, Folly Mills	Central Augusta	Staunton Beverley Manor Elementary School	20.0	—	1,175	76
	Fort Defiance						
19	Ft Defiance North—Damtown, New Hope, Piedmont, Knightly, Mt Sidney	North Augusta	Ft Defiance Elementary School	15.9	—	670	80
20	Ft Defiance South—Mt Pisgah, Quicks Mill, Verona, New Hope, Damtown	North Augusta	Ft Defiance Elementary School	20.2	—	930	83
	Craigsville						
21	Craigsville—Augusta Springs, Estaline, Ford-wick	Far Southwest Augusta	Craigsville Elementary School	14.7	—	745	87
	Waynesboro						
22	Waynesboro Northeast—Dooms	East Augusta	Waynesboro Ridgeview Park	15.0	—	715	91

RIDE NO.	RIDE NAME	REGION	START LOCATION	DISTANCE (MILES)	OPTIONS (MILES)	ELEVATION (FEET)	PAGE
23	Waynesboro North (long)—Madrid, Red Mills, Mt Meridian, Piedmont, New Hope, Kidville	East Augusta	Waynesboro Ridgeview Park	31.8	28, 25, 22	850	94
24	Waynesboro North (short)—Kidville, Hermitage, Madrid	East Augusta	Waynesboro Ridgeview Park	16.6	—	505	98
25	Waynesboro South (short)—Lyndhurst, Lipscomb	East Augusta	Waynesboro Coyner Springs Park	10.3	—	145	101
26	Waynesboro South (long)—Lyndhurst, Sherando, Lipscomb	East Augusta	Waynesboro Coyner Springs Park	15.7	—	325	104
	Stuarts Draft						
27	Stuarts Draft—Cold Spring, Spottswood, Greenville	Southeast Augusta	Stuarts Draft Town Park	35.8	19.5	1,415	107

	Albemarle County Charlottesville						
28	Charlottesville South—Red Hill, Dudley Mtn	Central Albemarle	Charlottesville Azalea Park	14.8	—	865	113
29	Charlottesville Northwest—Owensville, Farmington	Central Albemarle	Charlottesville Azalea Park	20.1	—	800	115
30	Charlottesville West—Red Hill, Taylors Gap, Bloomfield	Central Albemarle	Charlottesville Azalea Park	24.3	—	1,315	118
	Earlysville						
31	Earlysville Northwest (short)—Ehart, Nortons-ville	North Albemarle	Earlysville Broadus Wood Elementary School	13.3	—	500	122
32	Earlysville Northwest (long)—Free Union, Boonesville, Nortonsville	Northwest Albemarle	Earlysville Broadus Wood Elementary School	23.7	—	1,000	124
33	Earlysville South—Free Union, Rivanna Reservoir	North Central Albemarle	Earlysville Broadus Wood Elementary School	22.8	—	1,050	127

RIDE NO.	RIDE NAME	REGION	START LOCATION	DISTANCE (MILES)	OPTIONS (MILES)	ELEVATION (FEET)	PAGE
34	Earlysville West—Free Union, Boonesville, Mountfair, Whitehall, Owensville	Northwest Albemarle	Earlysville Broadus Wood Elementary School	40.2	—	1,850	130
35	Earlysville Northeast—Advanced Mills, Midway, Frays Mountain	North Albemarle/ South Greene	Earlysville Broadus Wood Elementary School	18.0	—	865	133
	Stony Point						
36	Stony Point—Burnley	Northeast Albemarle	Stony Point Elementary School	18.7	—	885	137
	Red Hill, Walnut Creek, and Carters Bridge						
37	Red Hill Northwest—Taylors Gap, Miller School, Batesville, Tom Mountain	West Albemarle	Red Hill Elementary School	18.4	—	1,325	141
38	Red Hill Southeast—South Garden, North Garden, Crossroads, Tom Mountain	Central Albemarle	Red Hill Elementary School	20.8	—	1,175	144

39	Walnut Creek Park—South Garden, Keene, Alberene	South Central Albemarle	Albemarle Walnut Creek Park	21.6	—	1,575	147
40	Carters Bridge—Overton, Blenheim	Southeast Albemarle	Albemarle Walton Middle School	16.7	12.5	640	150
	Esmont						
41	Esmont—Tapscott, Porter	South Albemarle	Esmont Simpson Park	15.9	—	650	153
	Greenwood						
42	Greenwood South—Newtown	West Albemarle	Greenwood Community Center	9.3	—	500	157
43	Greenwood Southwest—Newtown, Afton, Avon	West Albemarle/ North Nelson	Greenwood Community Center	22.2	—	1,465	160
	Greene County **Stanardsville**						
44	Stanardsville North—Brills Shop, South River	North Greene	Stanardsville William Monroe High School	22.0	16.1	1,040	164
45	Stanardsville South—Amicus, Geer	South Greene	Stanardsville William Monroe High School	15.6	—	710	167

Rockingham County

rides leaving from

Harrisonburg

Bridgewater and Dayton

Montevideo

Grottoes

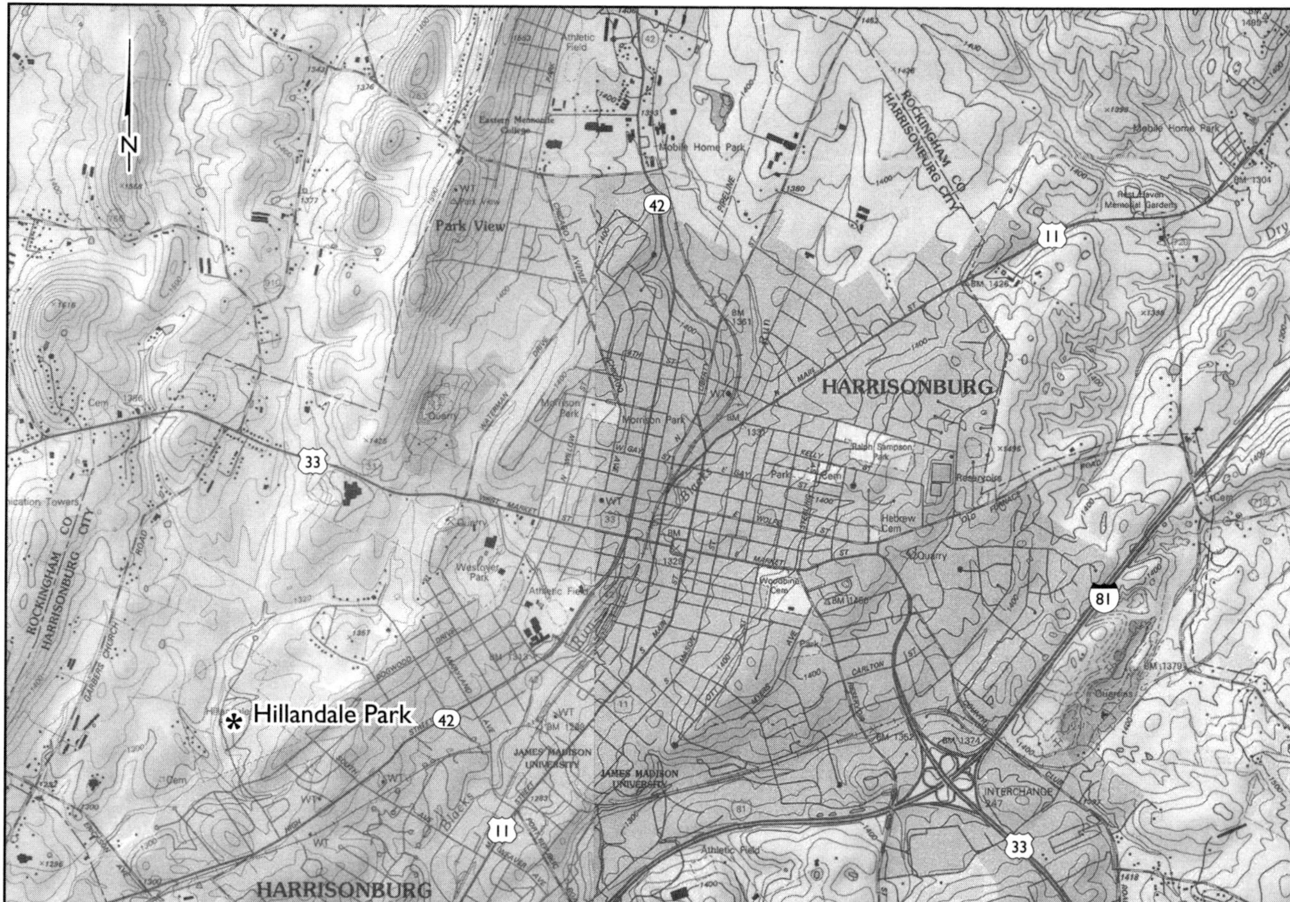

N
Hillandale Park
HARRISONBURG
HARRISONBURG
Park View
Eastern Mennonite College
Mobile Home Park
ROCKINGHAM CO
HARRISONBURG CITY
Rest Haven Memorial Gardens
Morrison Park
Ralph Sampson Park
Reservoirs
Hebrew Cem
Woodbine Cem
Westover Park
Athletic Field
JAMES MADISON UNIVERSITY
INTERCHANGE 247
42
11
33
81

Ride 1: Harrisonburg Northeast

Keezletown, Zenda

This lollipop-shaped ride heads out on a scenic loop of country roads to the east and northeast of Harrisonburg along the western base of Massanutten Mountain. The area is popular for riding among Harrisonburg locals. A shorter, approximately 18-mile ride eliminates the trek in and out of town and therefore cuts out most of the traffic.

DISTANCE 31.5 miles

ELEVATION CHANGE 1,620 feet

TRAFFIC LEVEL Medium to high in and just outside of Harrisonburg; low levels once out of town.

TERRAIN Typical rolling Shenandoah Valley terrain with hills that add up as the miles roll on.

STORES ALONG THE ROUTE None outside the Harrisonburg city limits.

START LOCATION Hillandale Park. From downtown Harrisonburg, travel south on Route 42 South High Street for about 1.5 miles. Turn right on Hillandale Drive, which turns into the park entrance after a few blocks.

COMMENTS This ride can be combined with other routes leaving Harrisonburg to make longer rides. Note: The return portion of this loop is the same as the outbound portion of the Harrisonburg North loop. For an 18-mile option, start and finish at the former Keezletown Elementary School at the junction of Route 717 Indian Trail and Route 620 Mountain Valley Road (point M).

POINT	MILES	DESCRIPTION
A	0.0	Exit Hillandale Park on Hillandale Dr
B	0.1	Left on Dogwood Dr
C	1.6	Cross Rt 33 W Market St
D	1.7	Right on Wolfe St
E	2.1	Cross Rt 42 High St
F	2.2	Cross Rt 11 N Liberty St
G	2.3	Cross Rt 11 Main St
H	3.0	Continue straight on Old Furnace Rd (becomes Rt 718)
I	3.3	Cross Vine St
J	4.2	Bear right on Rt 718 Old Furnace Rd
K	4.5	Cross I-81 (no interchange) and bear left on Rt 718 Old Furnace Rd
L	6.9	Right on Rt 717 Indian Trail

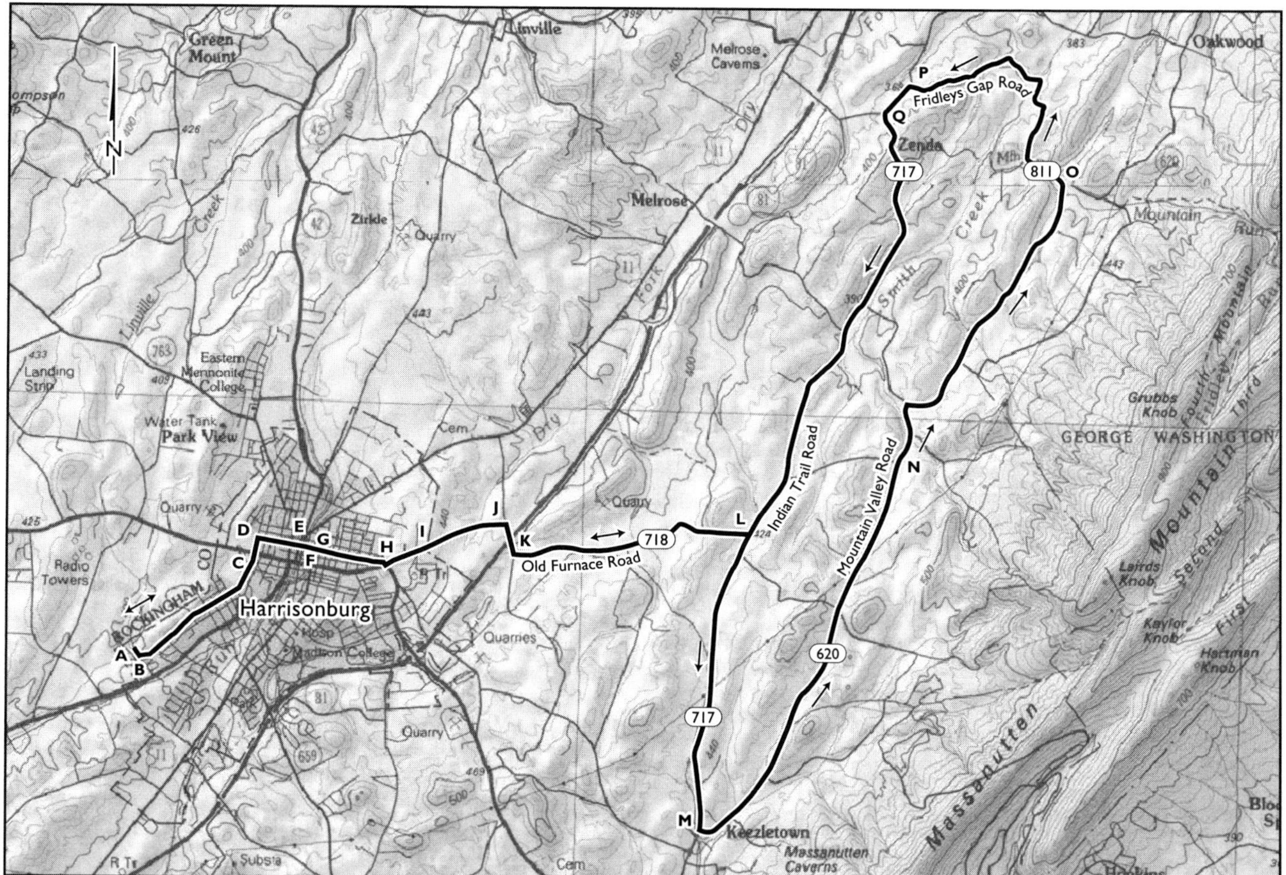

Harrisonburg
Old Furnace Road
Indian Trail Road
Mountain Valley Road
Fridleys Gap Road
717
718
620
811
A
B
C
D
E
F
G
H
I
J
K
L
M
N
O
P
Q
N
Green Mount
Linville
Melrose Caverns
Oakwood
Zenda
Melrose
Zirkle
Eastern Mennonite College
Landing Strip
Water Tank
Park View
Radio Towers
Rockingham
Madison College
Hosp
Quarries
Quarry
Keezletown
Massanutten Caverns
Massanutten
George Washington
Grubbs Knob
Lairds Knob
Kaylor Knob
Hartman Knob
Mountain
Smith Creek
Linville Creek
Dry Fork

Ride 1: Harrisonburg Northeast

POINT	MILES	DESCRIPTION
M	9.7	Left on Rt 620 Mountain Valley Rd. Former Keezletown Elementary School here
N	14.0	Continue straight on Rt 620
O	17.4	Left on Rt 811 Fridleys Gap Rd
P	20.0	Left on Rt 717 Indian Trail
Q	20.3	Bear left on Rt 717 Indian Trail
L	24.6	Right on Rt 718 Old Furnace Rd. If starting from former Keezletown Elementary School, continue straight here and head back to start
K	27.0	Bear right on Rt 718 Old Furnace Rd and cross I-81 (no interchange)
J	27.3	Bear left on Rt 718 Old Furnace Rd
I	28.2	Cross Vine St
H	28.5	Continue straight on Wolfe St
G	29.2	Cross Rt 11 Main St
F	29.3	Cross Rt 11 N Liberty St
E	29.4	Cross Rt 42 High St
D	29.8	Left on Dogwood Dr
C	29.9	Cross Rt 33 W Market St
B	31.4	Right on Hillandale Dr
A	31.5	Finish at Hillandale Park

Ride 2: Harrisonburg North

Zenda, Hightown, Linville, Edom, Green Mount

This hilly ride features plenty of delightful mountain scenery. Enjoy views of Massanutten Mountain on the way out as you head north along the Shenandoah Valley. On the return, ride a ridge road south along the center of the valley, where you can see Massanutten to the east and Shenandoah Mountain to the west.

DISTANCE 31.5 miles

ELEVATION CHANGE 1,735 feet

TRAFFIC LEVEL Medium to high in and just outside of Harrisonburg; low levels once out of town. Use caution when crossing Routes 11 and 42 and on Mount Clinton Pike, which is a busy secondary road.

TERRAIN Hilly.

STORES ALONG THE ROUTE None.

START LOCATION Hillandale Park. From downtown Harrisonburg, travel south on Route 42 South High Street for about 1.5 miles. Turn right on Hillandale Drive, which turns into the park entrance after a few blocks.

COMMENTS For a shorter route, beginners could ride out along the start and turn around as they please. For longer rides, combine this route with others leaving Harrisonburg. For example, riders could start on the Harrisonburg Northeast ride and switch to this one after Fridleys Gap Road (point M on this route; point Q on that route).

POINT	MILES	DESCRIPTION
A	0.0	Exit Hillandale Park on Hillandale Dr
B	0.1	Left on Dogwood Dr
C	1.6	Cross Rt 33 W Market St
D	1.7	Right on Wolfe St
E	2.1	Cross Rt 42 High St
F	2.2	Cross Rt 11 N Liberty St
G	2.3	Cross Rt 11 Main St
H	3.0	Continue straight on Old Furnace Rd (becomes Rt 718)
I	3.3	Cross Vine St
J	4.2	Bear right on Rt 718 Old Furnace Rd
—	4.5	Cross I-81 (no interchange) and bear left on Rt 718 Old Furnace Rd
K	6.9	Left on Rt 717 Indian Trail
L	7.6	Bear left continuing on Rt 717 Indian Trail

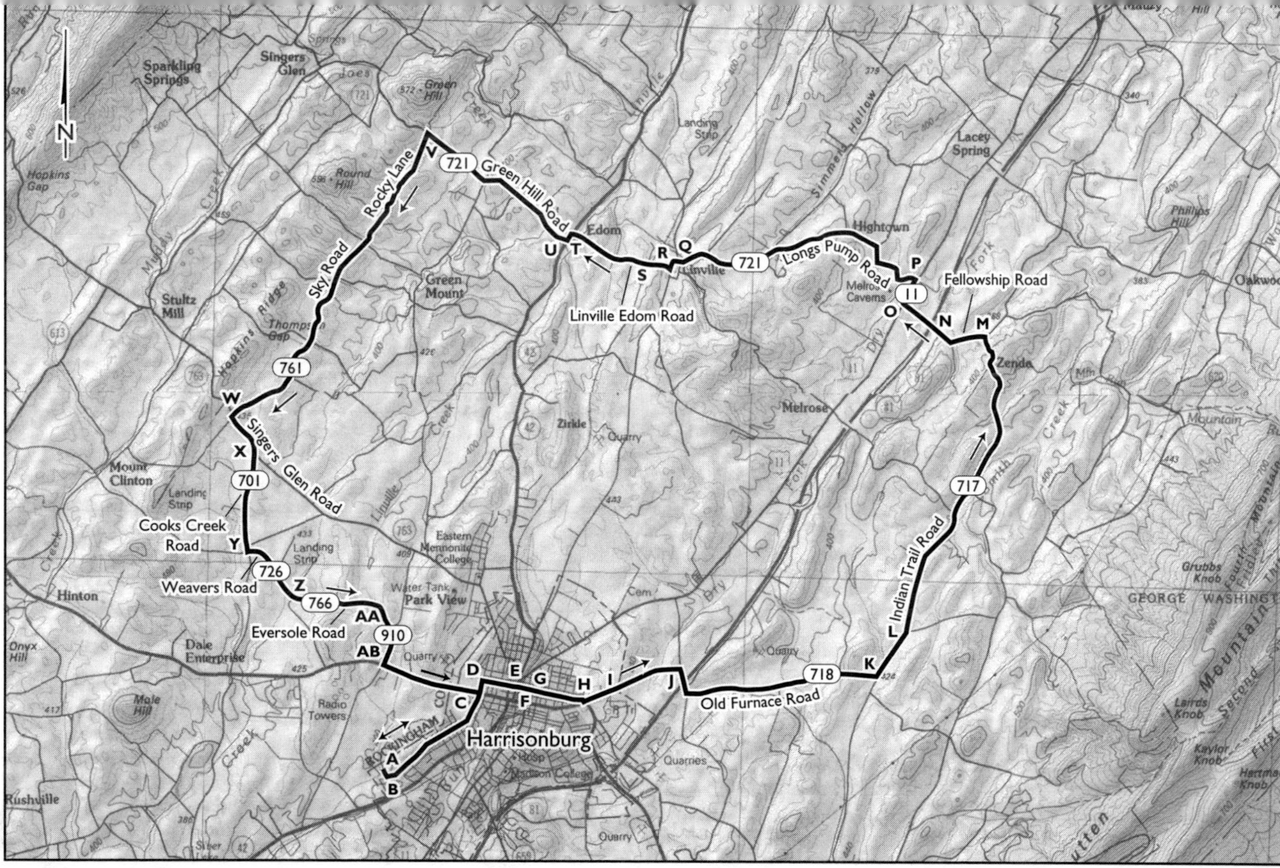

HARRISONBURG NORTH

Ride 2: Harrisonburg North

POINT	MILES	DESCRIPTION
M	11.6	Left on Rt 721 Fellowship Rd
N	12.3	Cross I-81 (no interchange)
O	12.8	Right on Rt 11 Valley Pike
P	13.0	Left on Rt 721 Longs Pump Rd
Q	16.5	Left on Rt 721 Kratzer Rd
R	16.6	Right on Rt 721 Linville Edom Rd
S	16.8	Cross railroad tracks
T	17.9	Left on Rt 42 Harpine Hwy
U	18.0	Right on Rt 721 Green Hill Rd
V	20.1	Left on Rt 761 Rocky Ln (becomes Sky Rd)
W	24.4	Left on Rt 763 Singers Glen Rd
X	25.0	Right on Rt 701 Cooks Creek Rd
Y	26.1	Straight on Rt 701 Mt Clinton Pike
—	26.2	Left on Rt 726 Weavers Rd
Z	27.0	Left on Rt 766 Eversole Rd
AA	28.3	Straight on Rt 910 Switchboard Rd
AB	28.7	Left on Rt 33 W Market St
C	29.9	Right on Dogwood Dr
B	31.4	Right on Hillandale Dr
A	31.5	Finish at Hillandale Park

Ride 3: Harrisonburg West

Dayton, Rushville, Clover Hill, Lilly, Mount Clinton

This ride travels through the heart of Mennonite farm country. You are likely to see horse-drawn buggies and Mennonite children riding bicycles. Along the way, you will pass Silver Lake and Silver Lake Mill, as well as the outskirts of Dayton. A section of the ride also covers the locally known "time trial road," which probably is the only truly flat section of road in the valley.

DISTANCE 25.0miles

ELEVATION CHANGE 1,500 feet

TRAFFIC LEVEL Medium to high in and just outside of Harrisonburg. Low levels once out of town, and almost no traffic on the small roads through Mennonite farm country. Use caution especially on and near Routes 33 and 42.

TERRAIN Typical rolling Shenandoah Valley terrain. There are hills, but you often get a good rolling start on the preceding downhills. One section of the ride is rather flat and good for time trial practice. Save energy for the end of the ride, which is more hilly than the beginning.

STORES ALONG THE ROUTE One, not long before crossing Route 33 Rawley Pike at about the midpoint of the ride.

START LOCATION Hillandale Park. From downtown Harrisonburg, travel south on Route 42 South High Street for about 1.5 miles. Turn right on Hillandale Drive, which turns into the park entrance after a few blocks.

COMMENTS For longer routes, this ride can be combined with others leaving Harrisonburg, particularly the Harrisonburg Northwest ride. It also overlaps with part of the Dayton ride.

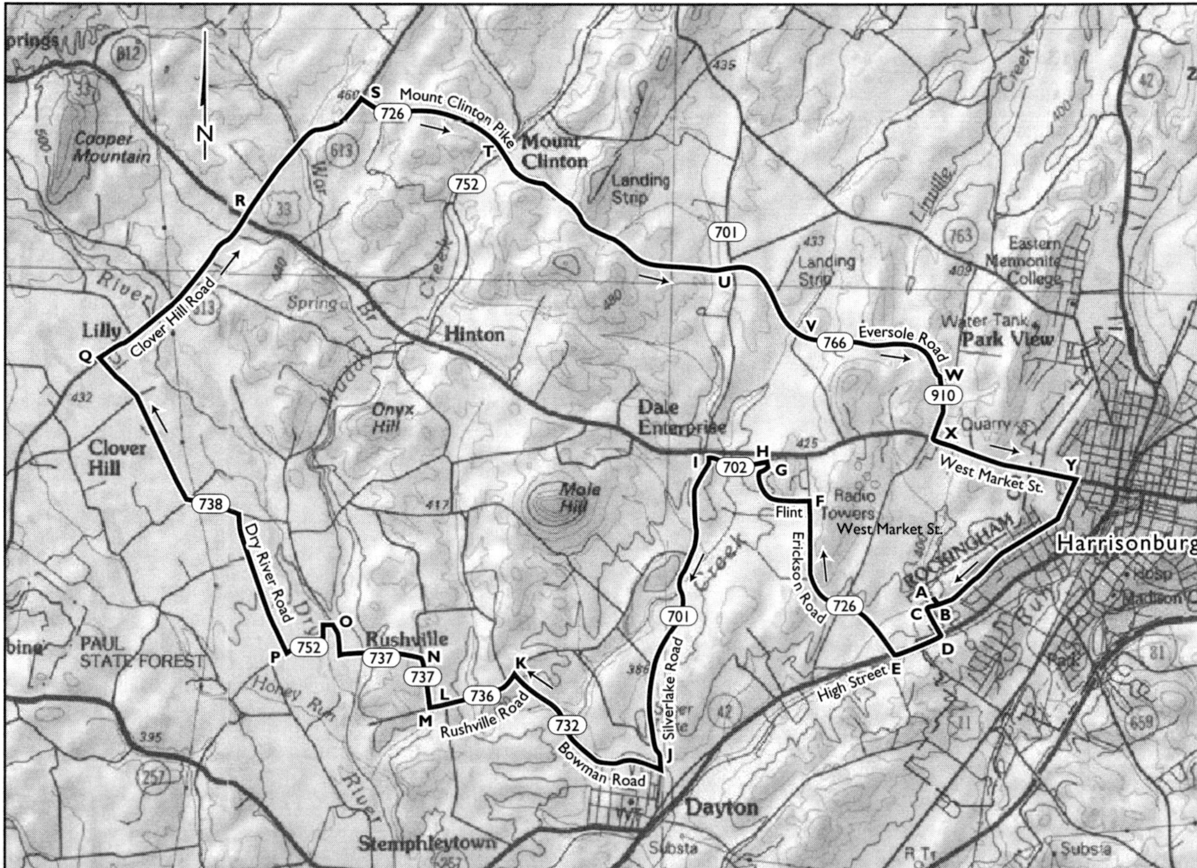

Mount Clinton Pike
Mount Clinton
Landing Strip
Cooper Mountain
Clover Hill Road
Lilly
Hinton
Onyx Hill
Dale Enterprise
Clover Hill
Mole Hill
Dry River Road
Rushville
PAUL STATE FOREST
Rushville Road
Bowman Road
Silverlake Road
Dayton
Stemphleytown
Eversole Road
Park View
Water Tank
Eastern Mennonite College
West Market St.
Radio Towers
Flint
Erickson Road
Harrisonburg
ROCKINGHAM
High Street

Ride 3: Harrisonburg West

POINT	MILES	DESCRIPTION
A	0.0	Exit Hillandale Park on Hillandale Dr
B	0.1	Right on Dogwood Dr
C	0.3	Left on Hidden Creek Ln
D	0.6	Right on Rt 42 S High St
E	0.9	Right on Rt 726 Erickson Rd
F	2.4	Left on Flint Ave
G	3.1	Left on Belmont Dr
H	3.2	Left on Rt 702 Old Rt 33
I	3.6	Left on Rt 701 Silverlake Rd
J	6.2	Right on Rt 732 Bowman Rd
K	7.8	Left on Rt 736 Rushville Rd
L	8.5	Straight on Rt 737/Rt 736 Rushville Rd
M	8.6	Right on Rt 737 Rushville Rd
N	9.0	Left on Rt 737 Rushville Rd
O	9.8	Left on Rt 752 Rushville Rd
P	10.2	Right on Rt 738 Dry River Rd
Q	13.2	Right on Rt 613 Clover Hill Rd
—	13.5	Store here
R	14.8	Cross Rt 33 Rawley Pike
S	16.2	Right on Rt 726 Mt Clinton Pike
T	17.5	Cross Rt 752
U	19.7	Cross Rt 701. Rt 726 becomes Weavers Rd
V	20.5	Left on Rt 766 Eversole Rd
W	21.8	Straight on Rt 910 Switchboard Rd
X	22.2	Left on Rt 33 W Market St
Y	23.4	Right on Dogwood Dr
B	24.9	Right on Hillandale Dr
A	25.0	Finish at Hillandale Park

Ride 4: Harrisonburg Northwest

Green Mount, Singers Glen, Sparkling Springs, Stultz Mill, Mount Clinton

This hilly ride features roads through farmlands and to historic Singers Glen. Riders approach the eastern edge of George Washington National Forest as they leave Singers Glen and climb to the base of Shenandoah Mountain. The ride also features a delightful one-lane paved farm road through Mount Clinton. There is an option of about 18 miles for riders seeking less distance.

DISTANCE 35.5 miles

ELEVATION CHANGE 1,920 feet

TRAFFIC LEVEL Medium to high in and just outside of Harrisonburg. Low levels once out of town, but use caution on busy Singers Glen Road and Mount Clinton Pike.

TERRAIN Some steep climbs may seem tough for beginners. Expect constant rolling hills and little flat terrain.

STORES ALONG THE ROUTE One, about one-third of the way through.

START LOCATION Hillandale Park. From downtown Harrisonburg, travel south on Route 42 South High Street for about 1.5 miles. Turn right on Hillandale Drive, which turns into the park entrance after a few blocks.

COMMENTS Because of this ride's hilliness and length, some riders may wish to cut it to 18 miles. To do so, turn left on Route 772 Greenmount Road (point K) instead of crossing it. One mile later, turn left again on Route 761 Sky Road (point Z) and follow the rest of the route as described.

POINT	MILES	DESCRIPTION
A	0.0	Exit Hillandale Park on Hillandale Dr
B	0.1	Right on Dogwood Dr
C	0.3	Left on Hidden Creek Ln
D	0.6	Right on Rt 42 S High St
E	0.9	Right on Rt 726 Ericson Rd
F	1.5	Right on Rt 910 Garbers Church Rd
G	3.0	Cross Rt 33 W Market St. Rt 910 becomes Switchboard Rd
H	3.5	Right on Rt 910 Switchboard Rd
I	4.5	Right on Rt 763 Mt Clinton Pike
J	4.7	Left on Rt 910 Ft Lynne Rd
K	7.8	Cross Rt 772 Greenmount Rd. Rt 910 becomes Grist Mill Rd. Turn left here for shortcut

HARRISONBURG NORTHWEST

Ride 4: Harrisonburg Northwest

POINT	MILES	DESCRIPTION
L	9.6	Left on Rt 721 Green Hill Rd
M	11.5	Left on Rt 721 Green Hill Rd
N	12.3	Straight on Rt 613 Singers Glen Rd. Store soon after intersection
O	13.9	Right on Rt 772 Sparkling Springs Rd
P	15.1	Left on Rt 773 Sparkling Springs Rd (becomes Chrisman Rd). Sparkling Springs Rd soon turns off to right
Q	16.2	Straight on Rt 771 Chrisman Rd
R	17.7	Right on Rt 613 Singers Glen Rd
S	18.1	Right on Rt 763 Whitmore Shop Rd
T	18.7	Left on Rt 613 Whitmore Shop Rd
U	19.7	Left on Rt 760 Custers Rd
V	21.3	Left on Rt 726 Mt Clinton Pike
W	21.4	Left on Rt 752 Muddy Creek Rd
X	23.4	Left on Rt 763 Singers Glen Rd
—	23.5	Right on Rt 752 Snapps Creek Rd
Y	25.0	Right on Rt 772 Greenmount Rd
Z	26.2	Right on Rt 761 Sky Rd. Shortcut rejoins here
AA	28.4	Left on Rt 763 Singers Glen Rd
AB	29.0	Right on Rt 701 Cooks Creek Rd
AC	30.1	Straight on Rt 701 Mt Clinton Pike
—	30.2	Left on Rt 726 Weavers Rd
AD	31.0	Left on Rt 766 Eversole Rd
H	32.3	Straight on Rt 910 Switchboard Rd
G	32.7	Left on Rt 33 W Market St
AE	33.9	Right on Dogwood Dr
B	35.4	Right on Hillandale Dr
A	35.5	Finish at Hillandale Park

BRIDGEWATER AND DAYTON AREA

Ride 5: Dayton

Rushville, Hinton, Mole Hill

Pass through Mennonite farm country on this short ride, which features quiet back roads. You will see many gravel roads turning off along the way. Most of the climbing happens in the first two-thirds of the ride, culminating with a trip toward the summit of Mole Hill. Enjoy nice views on the way up and the rest of the mostly downhill trip back past Silver Lake.

DISTANCE 12.5miles

ELEVATION CHANGE 745 feet

TRAFFIC LEVEL Low.

TERRAIN Typical rolling Shenandoah Valley hills with one big, steep climb up Mole Hill. The effort is rewarded with a nice downhill that takes you most of the way back.

STORES ALONG THE ROUTE None.

START LOCATION Cooks Creek Park. If the parking area is full, park across the street at the Harrisonburg/Rockingham Historical Society. From Harrisonburg, go south on Route 42 for just under four miles. Just before Dayton, turn right on Business Route 42 South. Turn right on Route 732. Turn left for a brief stretch on College Road, then take a quick right onto Route 732 Bowman Avenue. Cooks Creek Park is on the right almost immediately after the intersection.

COMMENTS This is a great ride for beginners because of the short distance and low traffic levels. The climb up Mole Hill is tough, but it's the only one like it on the route. If you're feeling adventurous, explore the many interconnecting gravel roads in the area.

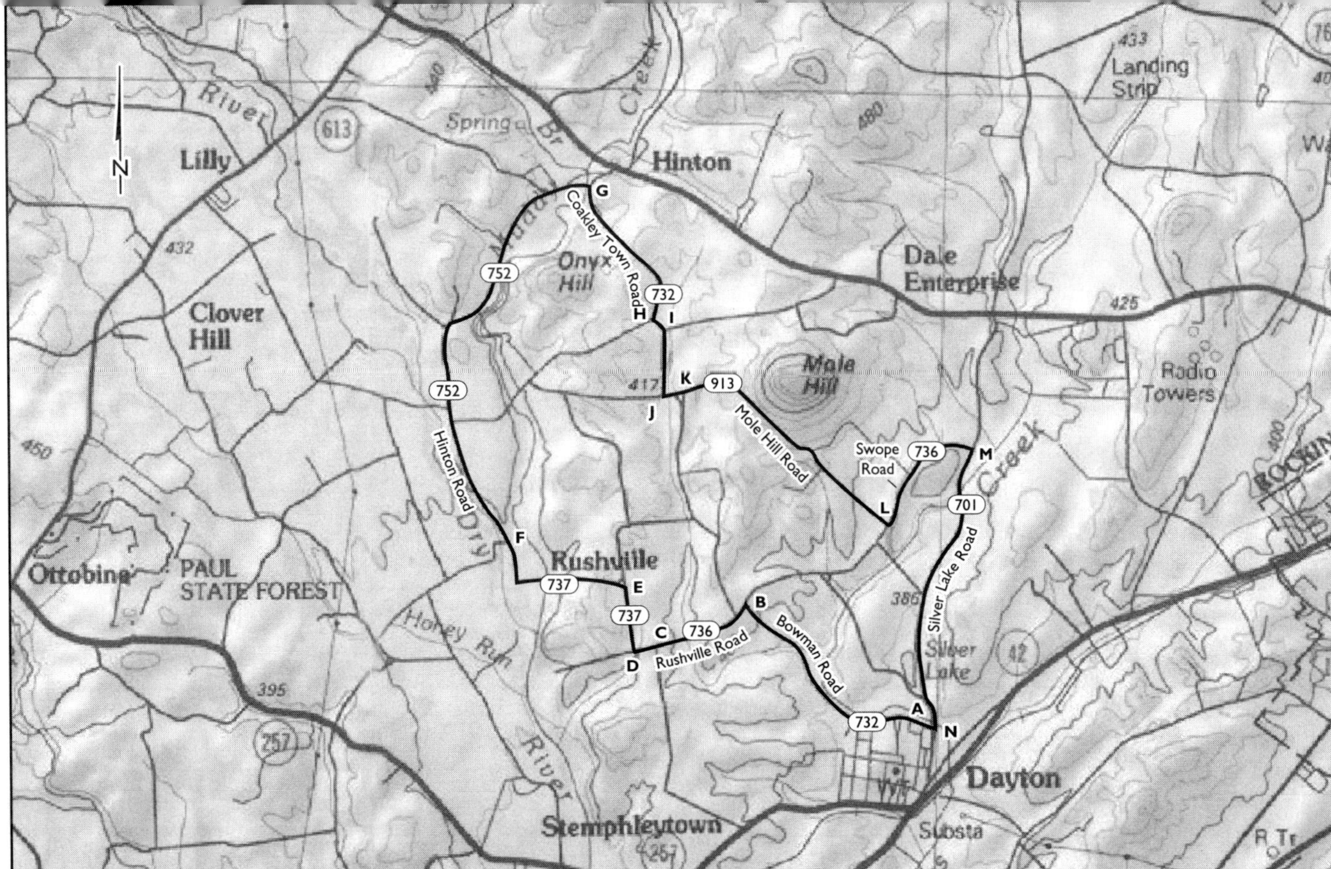

N
Lilly
Hinton
Clover Hill
Onyx Hill
Dale Enterprise
Mole Hill
Radio Towers
Landing Strip
Rushville
Ottobine
PAUL STATE FOREST
Stemphleytown
Dayton
Silver Lake
Coakley Town Road
Hinton Road
Mole Hill Road
Swope Road
Silver Lake Road
Rushville Road
Bowman Road
752
732
913
736
701
737
613
257
42
A
B
C
D
E
F
G
H
I
J
K
L
M
N

DAYTON

Ride 5: Dayton

POINT	MILES	DESCRIPTION
A	0.0	Exit Cooks Creek Park by turning right on Rt 732 Bowman Rd
B	1.5	Left on Rt 736/732 Rushville Rd
C	2.1	Straight on Rt 737 Rushville Rd
D	2.3	Right on Rt 737 Rushville Rd
E	2.7	Left on Rt 737 Rushville Rd
F	3.5	Straight on Rt 752 Hinton Rd
G	6.4	Right on Rt 732 Coakley Town Rd
H	7.5	Bear left continuing on Rt 732 Coakley Town Rd. Rt 734 turns off to the right
I	7.6	Continue on Rt 732 Coakley Town Rd. Rt 734 turns off to the left
J	8.0	Left on Rt 732 Coakley Town Rd
K	8.1	Left on Rt 913 Mole Hill Rd
L	9.7	Left on Rt 736 Swope Rd
M	10.5	Right on Rt 701 Silver Lake Rd
—	11.9	Pass Silver Lake
N	12.4	Right on Rt 732 Bowman Rd
B/A	12.5	Finish at Cooks Creek Park on the right

Ride 6: Bridgewater Southwest

Spring Creek, Sangerville, Stokesville, Mount Solon, Mossy Creek, Centerville

The area southwest of Bridgewater offers some of the best riding and scenery in the Shenandoah Valley. Riders can enjoy unusual flat stretches as well as expansive views of the mountains at the edge of George Washington National Forest. Those up for sight-seeing can take side trips to Todd Lake or Natural Chimneys. Mountain bikers will smile as they pass through Stokesville, knowing some of the best riding on the East Coast lies just beyond in the national forest.

DISTANCE 28.4miles

ELEVATION CHANGE 1,060 feet

TRAFFIC LEVEL Moderate to heavy in Bridgewater; low levels outside of town.

TERRAIN Rolling Shenandoah Valley terrain with some unusually flat sections near Sangerville and Stokesville, making this ride relatively less hilly than others of the same length in this book.

STORES ALONG THE ROUTE Three.

START LOCATION Wildwood Park . From I-81, exit at Bridgewater/Mount Crawford (exit 240). Travel west on Route 257 toward Bridgewater. Turn left on Route 42 South. Turn right on West Bank Street. Turn left on Bank Street at T (Pope Street goes right). Road ends at Wildwood Park on the left.

COMMENTS Any of the rides from Bridgewater can be combined to make longer loops. Coming back to Bridgewater between loops gives the rider the opportunity to restock on food or water.

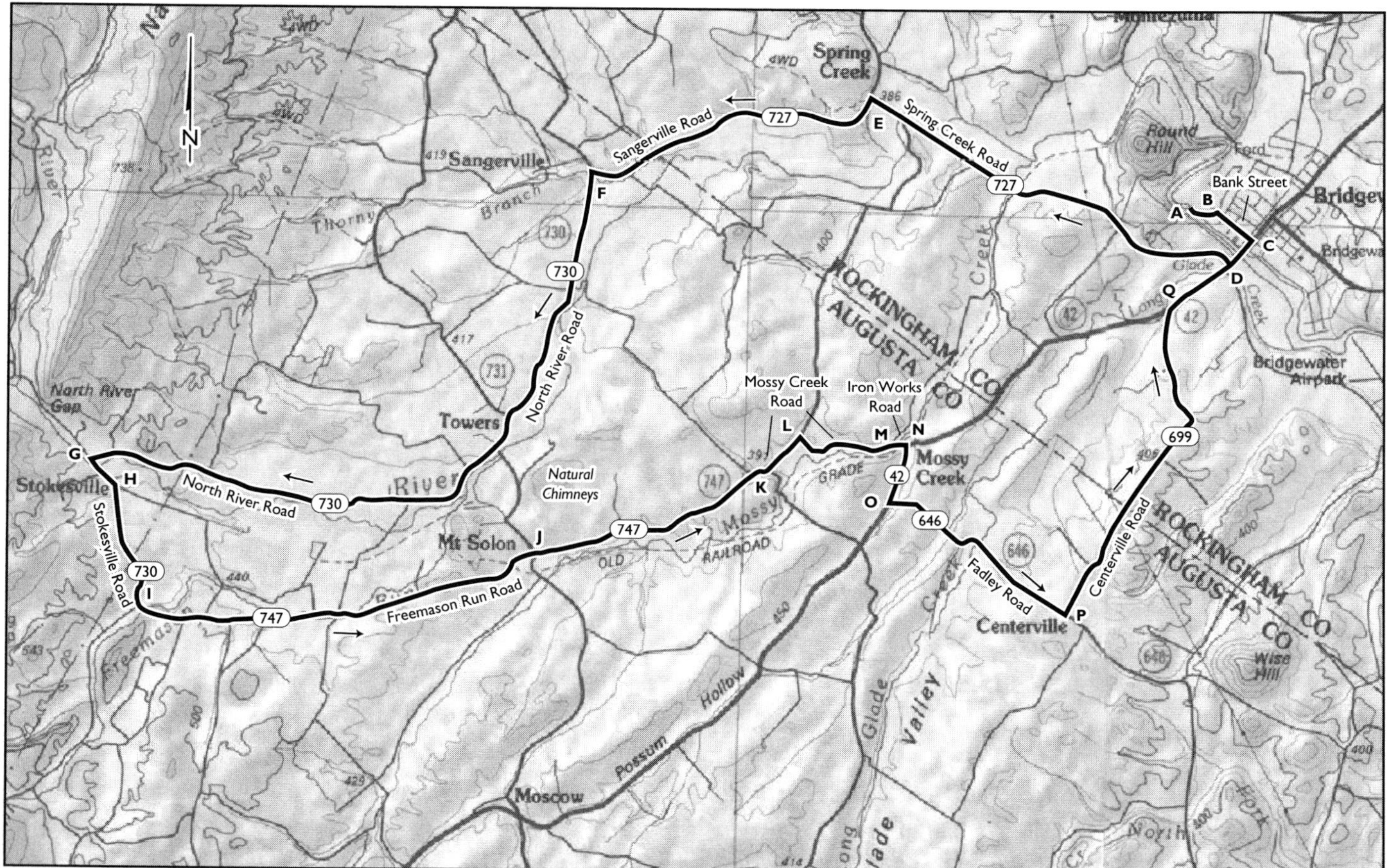

BRIDGEWATER SOUTHWEST

Ride 6: Bridgewater Southwest

POINT	MILES	DESCRIPTION
A	0.0	Exit Wildwood Park on Bank St heading back toward Bridgewater
B	0.2	Right on Bank St at stop sign
C	0.6	Right on Rt 42 Main St and cross bridge
D	0.8	Right on Rt 727 Spring Creek Rd
E	4.3	Left on Rt 727 Sangerville Rd
F	7.0	Left on Rt 730 North River Rd. Store here, and another just before the next intersection
G	13.2	Left on Rt 730 Stokesville Rd and cross one-lane bridge. Todd Lake is to the right four miles for riders looking for a picnic spot
H	13.5	Right on Rt 730 Stokesville Rd
I	14.5	Left on Rt 747 Freemason Run Rd and continue through subsequent intersections to Mt Solon
J	18.1	Cross Rt 731 Natural Chimneys Rd at Mt Solon. Turn left here and follow the signs to visit Natural Chimneys. Store here

POINT	MILES	DESCRIPTION
K	20.3	Straight on Rt 747 Mossy Creek Rd
L	20.7	Bear right continuing on Mossy Creek Rd
M	21.4	Straight on Rt 809 Iron Works Rd and cross bridge
N	21.6	Right on Rt 42 Scenic Hwy
O	22.1	Left on Rt 646 Fadley Rd
P	23.9	Left on Rt 699 Centerville Rd
Q	26.9	Right on Rt 42 Warm Springs Pike
C	27.8	Left on W Bank St
B	28.2	Left on Bank St toward park
A	28.4	Finish at Wildwood Park

Ride 7: Bridgewater Southeast

Airport, Burketown, North River

This ride has many climbs and descents as you cross farmlands covering the Shenandoah Valley's smaller longitudinal ridges. You will also enjoy a lovely section of road tucked away along the North River after viewing the Blue Ridge to the east for much of the ride.

DISTANCE 27.0 miles

ELEVATION CHANGE 1,150 feet

TRAFFIC LEVEL Moderate to heavy in Bridgewater; low levels outside of town. Use caution when on or crossing Routes 11, 42, 276, and 257, which are busy secondary roads.

TERRAIN Plenty of long, rolling hills, with some flatter sections along ridges and the North River.

STORES ALONG THE ROUTE None.

START LOCATION Wildwood Park . From I-81, exit at Bridgewater/Mount Crawford (exit 240). Travel west on Route 257 toward Bridgewater. Turn left on Route 42 South. Turn right on West Bank Street. Turn left on Bank Street at T (Pope Street goes right). Road ends at Wildwood Park on the left.

COMMENTS Any of the rides from Bridgewater can be combined to make longer loops. Coming back to Bridgewater between loops gives the rider the opportunity to restock on food or water.

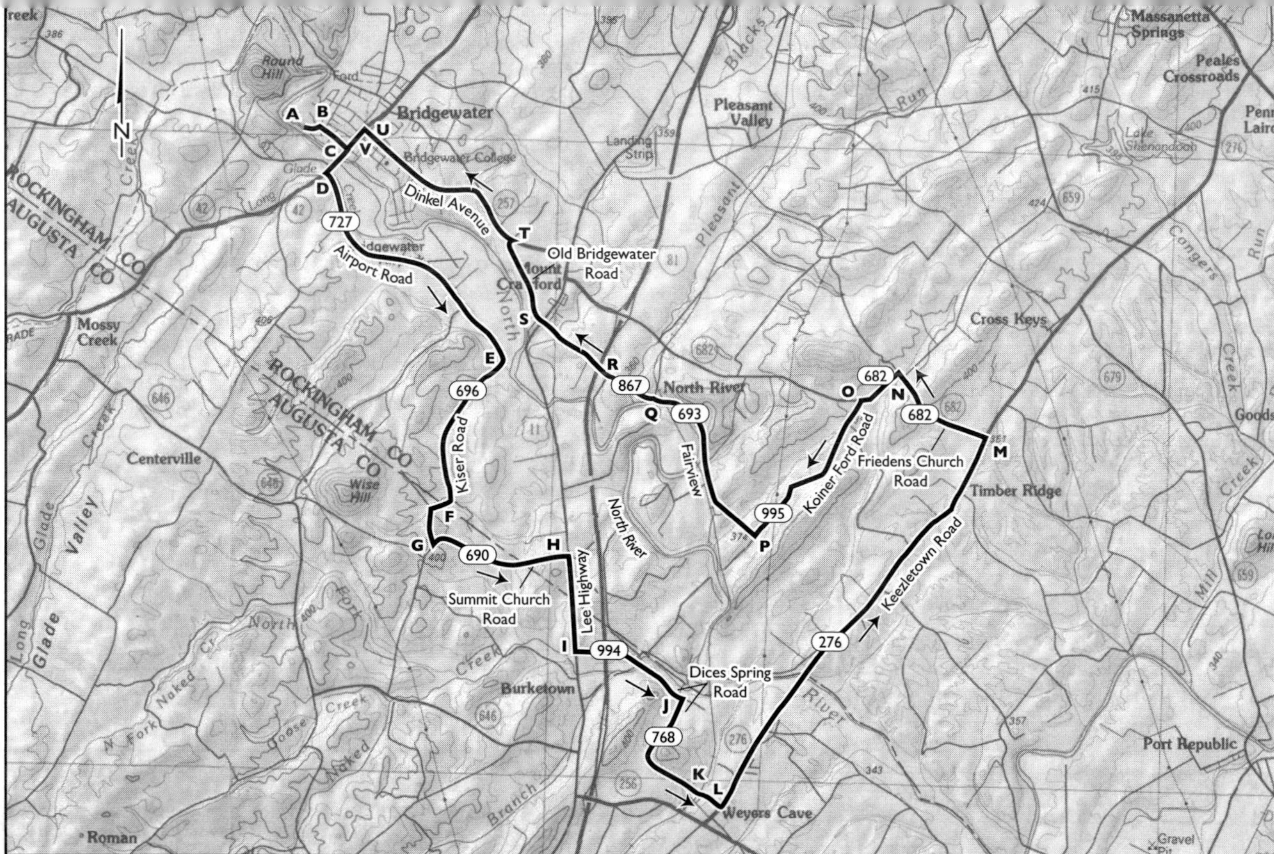

BRIDGEWATER SOUTHEAST

Ride 7: Bridgewater Southeast

POINT	MILES	DESCRIPTION
A	0.0	Exit Wildwood Park on Bank St heading back toward Bridgewater
B	0.2	Right on Bank St at stop sign
C	0.6	Right on Rt 42 Main St and cross bridge
D	0.9	Left on Rt 727 Airport Rd
E	3.8	Right on Rt 696 Kiser Rd
F	5.5	Continue around sharp bend to the right on Rt 696 Cratan Hill Rd
G	6.1	Left on Rt 690 Summit Church Rd
H	7.6	Right on Rt 11 Lee Hwy
I	8.5	Left on Rt 994 Dices Spring Rd. Cross I-81 (no interchange)
J	9.8	Right on Rt 768 Dices Spring Rd
K	11.2	Cross railroad tracks
L	11.5	Left on Rt 276 Keezletown Rd
M	16.2	Left on Rt 682 Friedens Church Rd
N	17.4	Left on Rt 682 Friedens Church Rd
O	17.9	Left on Rt 995 Koiner Ford Rd
P	19.8	Right on Rt 693 Fairview Rd
Q	21.7	Bear left on Rt 867 North River Rd
R	22.4	Cross I-81 (no interchange)
S	23.2	Cross Rt 11 Lee Hwy. Rt 867 becomes Old Bridgewater Rd
T	24.1	Left on Rt 257 Dinkel Ave
U	26.0	Left on 1st St
V	26.2	Road curves right on Bank St
C	26.4	Cross Rt 42 S Main St
B	26.8	Left on Bank St toward park
A	27.0	Finish at Wildwood Park

Ride 8: Bridgewater South

Airport, Centerville

On this short spin you'll pass the small Bridgewater airport and then head into the rolling farmlands of southern Rockingham and northern Augusta Counties. From the ridge out of Centerville, enjoy the views of the mountains. This ride is appropriate for beginners or can serve as an easy route for more experienced riders.

DISTANCE 13.5 miles

ELEVATION CHANGE 515 feet

TRAFFIC LEVEL Moderate to heavy in Bridgewater; low levels outside of town.

STORES ALONG THE ROUTE None.

START LOCATION Wildwood Park. From I-81, exit at Bridgewater/Mount Crawford (exit 240). Travel west on Route 257 toward Bridgewater. Turn left on Route 42 South. Turn right on West Bank Street. Turn left on Bank Street at T (Pope Street goes right). Road ends at Wildwood Park on the left.

COMMENTS Any of the rides from Bridgewater can be combined to make longer loops. Coming back to Bridgewater between loops gives the rider the opportunity to restock on food or water.

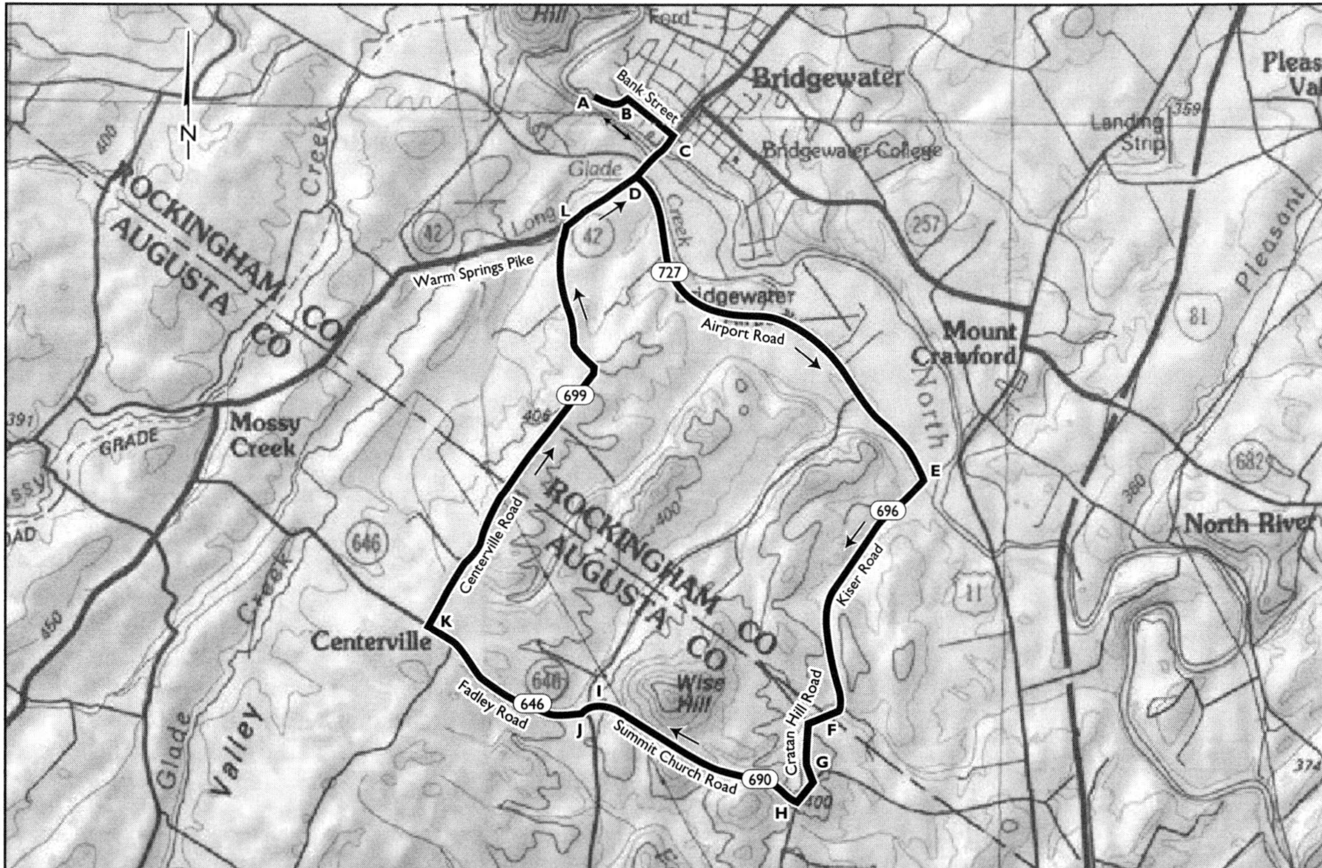

Bridgewater
Bank Street
Bridgewater College
Landing Strip
Pleasant Valley
N
ROCKINGHAM CO
AUGUSTA CO
Glade
Creek
Long
Warm Springs Pike
Bridgewater
Airport Road
Mount Crawford
North
North River
Pleasant
Mossy Creek
GRADE
Centerville Road
Kiser Road
Centerville
Wise Hill
Fadley Road
Summit Church Road
Cratan Hill Road
Glade
Valley
Creek
727
699
696
646
690
42
257
81
11
682
A
B
C
D
E
F
G
H
I
J
K
L

Ride 8: Bridgewater South

POINT	MILES	DESCRIPTION
A	0.0	Exit Wildwood Park on Bank St heading back toward Bridgewater
B	0.2	Right on Bank St at stop sign
C	0.6	Right on Rt 42 Main St and cross bridge
D	0.9	Left on Rt 727 Airport Rd
E	3.8	Right on Rt 696 Kiser Rd
F	5.5	Continue around sharp bend to the right on Rt 696 Cratan Hill Rd
G	6.1	Bear right on Rt 690 Summit Church Rd
H	6.3	Continue straight on Rt 690 Summit Church Rd
I	7.8	Bear left on Rt 690 Summit Church Rd
J	7.9	Right on Rt 646 Fadley Rd
K	9.0	Right on Rt 699 Centerville Rd
L	12.0	Right on Rt 42 Warm Springs Pike
C	12.9	Left on W Bank St
B	13.3	Left on Bank St toward park
A	13.5	Finish at Wildwood Park

Ride 9: Bridgewater Northwest

Clover Hill, Union Springs, Briery Branch, Spring Creek, Montezuma

Explore the quiet countryside northwest of Bridgewater and southwest of Harrisonburg while enjoying almost constant views of the mountains to the west. Wind through Mennonite farm country and cornfields to the base of the famous Reddish Knob paved climb. Enjoy a flat section known locally as the "time trial road."

DISTANCE 24.8 miles

ELEVATION CHANGE 750 feet

TRAFFIC LEVEL Moderate to heavy in Bridgewater; low levels outside of town.

TERRAIN Typical rolling Shenandoah Valley terrain with a few flat sections thrown in. This ride is flatter overall than many of the other valley rides.

STORES ALONG THE ROUTE One, at the midpoint of the route at the intersection of Briery Branch Road and Daniels Cupp Road in Briery Branch.

START LOCATION Wildwood Park . From I-81, exit at Bridgewater/Mount Crawford (exit 240). Travel west on Route 257 toward Bridgewater. Turn left on Route 42 South. Turn right on West Bank Street. Turn left on Bank Street at T (Pope Street goes right). Road ends at Wildwood Park on the left.

COMMENTS Any of the rides from Bridgewater can be combined to make longer loops. Coming back to Bridgewater between loops gives the rider the opportunity to restock on food or water.

POINT	MILES	DESCRIPTION
A	0.0	Exit Wildwood Park on Bank St heading back toward Bridgewater
B	0.2	Bear left/straight on Pope St at stop sign
C	0.5	Right on Green St
D	0.6	Left on View St
E	0.8	Right on North River Rd
F	1.1	Left on Dry River Rd (becomes Rt 738)
G	2.7	Left on Rt 257 Ottobine Rd and cross bridge
H	2.9	Right on Rt 738 Dry River Rd
I	4.9	Right on Rt 752 Keller Rd
J	5.0	Left on Rt 738 Dry River Rd
K	6.2	Left continuing on Rt 738 Dry River Rd

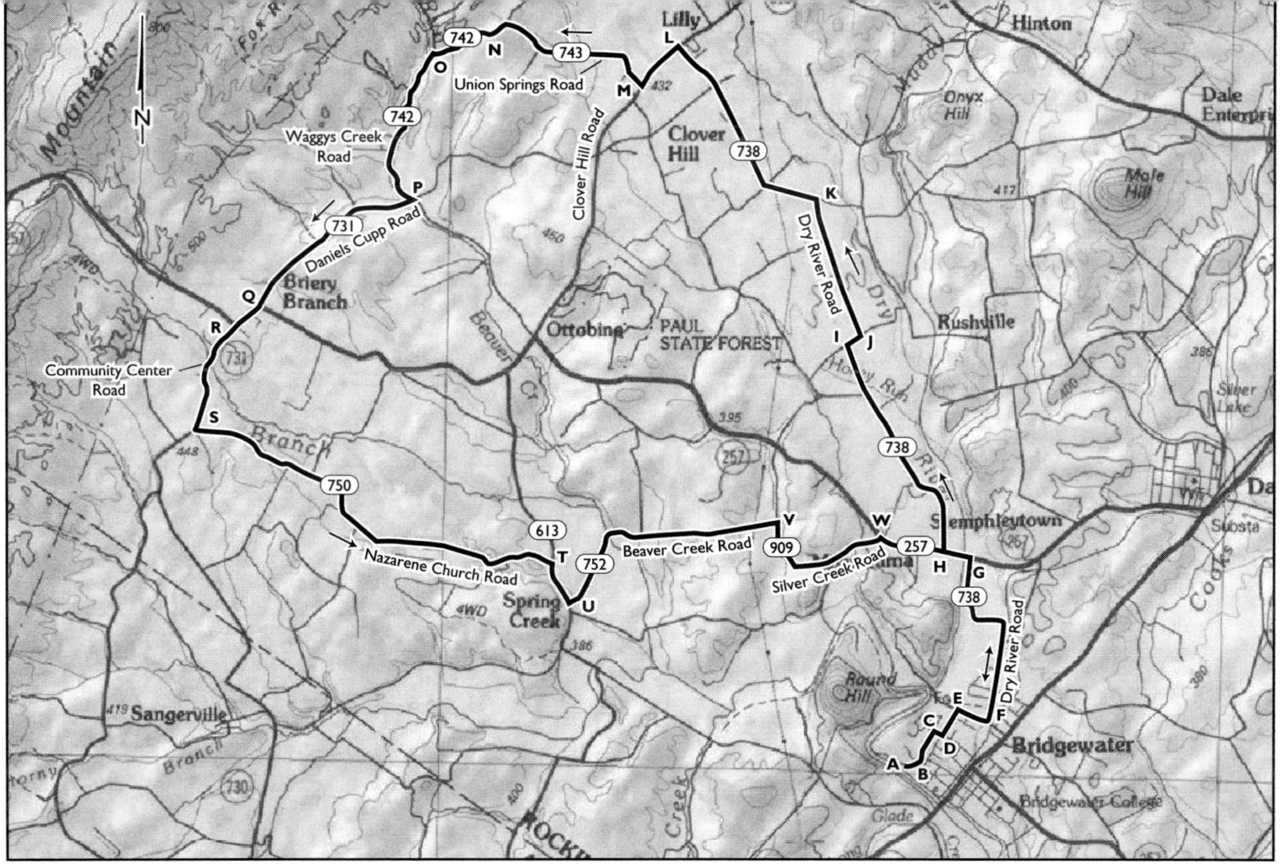

BRIDGEWATER NORTHWEST

Ride 9: Bridgewater Northwest

POINT	MILES	DESCRIPTION
L	8.0	Left on Rt 613 Clover Hill Rd
M	8.4	Right on Rt 743 Union Springs Rd
N	9.7	Left on Rt 742 Union Springs Rd
O	10.4	Bear left on Rt 742 Waggys Creek Rd
P	11.8	Right on Rt 731 Daniels Cupp Rd
Q	13.4	Right on Rt 731/257 Briery Branch Rd
R	13.6	Straight on Rt 731 Community Center Rd. Store here
S	14.5	Left on Rt 750 Nazarene Church Rd
T	18.0	Right on Rt 613 Spring Creek Rd
U	18.3	Left on Rt 752 Beaver Creek Rd
V	20.3	Right on Rt 909 Silver Creek Rd
W	21.6	Right on Rt 257 Ottobine Rd
G	22.3	Right on Rt 738 Dry River Rd
F	24.0	Right on North River Rd
E	24.2	Left on View St
D	24.5	Right on Green St
C	24.6	Left on Pope St
B	24.8	Bear right/straight onto W Bank St
A	25.0	Finish at Wildwood Park

Ride 10: Bridgewater East

North River, Cross Keys, Pleasant Valley

Experience a peaceful section of road along the North River before heading into farm country. Visit the 1862 Cross Keys Civil War Battlefield, then notice the march of time as you head back to Bridgewater through a more industrial area of the valley.

DISTANCE 24.9 miles

ELEVATION CHANGE 930 feet

TRAFFIC LEVEL Moderate to heavy in Bridgewater; low levels outside of town. Use caution when on or crossing Routes 11, 42, 276, and 257, which are busy secondary roads.

TERRAIN Rolling Shenandoah Valley terrain, but less hilly overall than some mid-valley rides.

STORES ALONG THE ROUTE One, by Route 11 about four miles before the finish.

START LOCATION Wildwood Park . From I-81, exit at Bridgewater/Mount Crawford (exit 240). Travel west on Route 257 toward Bridgewater. Turn left on Route 42 South. Turn right on West Bank Street. Turn left on Bank Street at T (Pope Street goes right). Road ends at Wildwood Park on the left.

COMMENTS Any of the rides from Bridgewater can be combined to make longer loops. Coming back to Bridgewater between loops gives the rider the opportunity to restock on food or water.

POINT	MILES	DESCRIPTION
A	0.0	Exit Wildwood Park on Bank St heading back toward Bridgewater
B	0.2	Right on Bank St at stop sign
C	0.6	Cross Rt 42 Main St
D	0.8	Left on First St (road curves)
E	1.0	Right on Rt 257 Dinkel Ave
F	2.9	Right on Rt 867 Old Bridgewater Rd
G	3.8	Cross Rt 11 Lee Hwy. Rt 867 becomes North River Rd. Cross I-81 (no interchange)
H	5.3	Bear right on Rt 693 Fairview Rd
I	7.2	Left on Rt 995 Koiners Ford Rd
J	9.1	Right on Rt 682 Friedens Church Rd
K	9.6	Right on Rt 682 Friedens Church Rd
L	10.8	Left on Rt 276 Cross Keys Rd
M	11.1	Right on Rt 671 Williams Rd

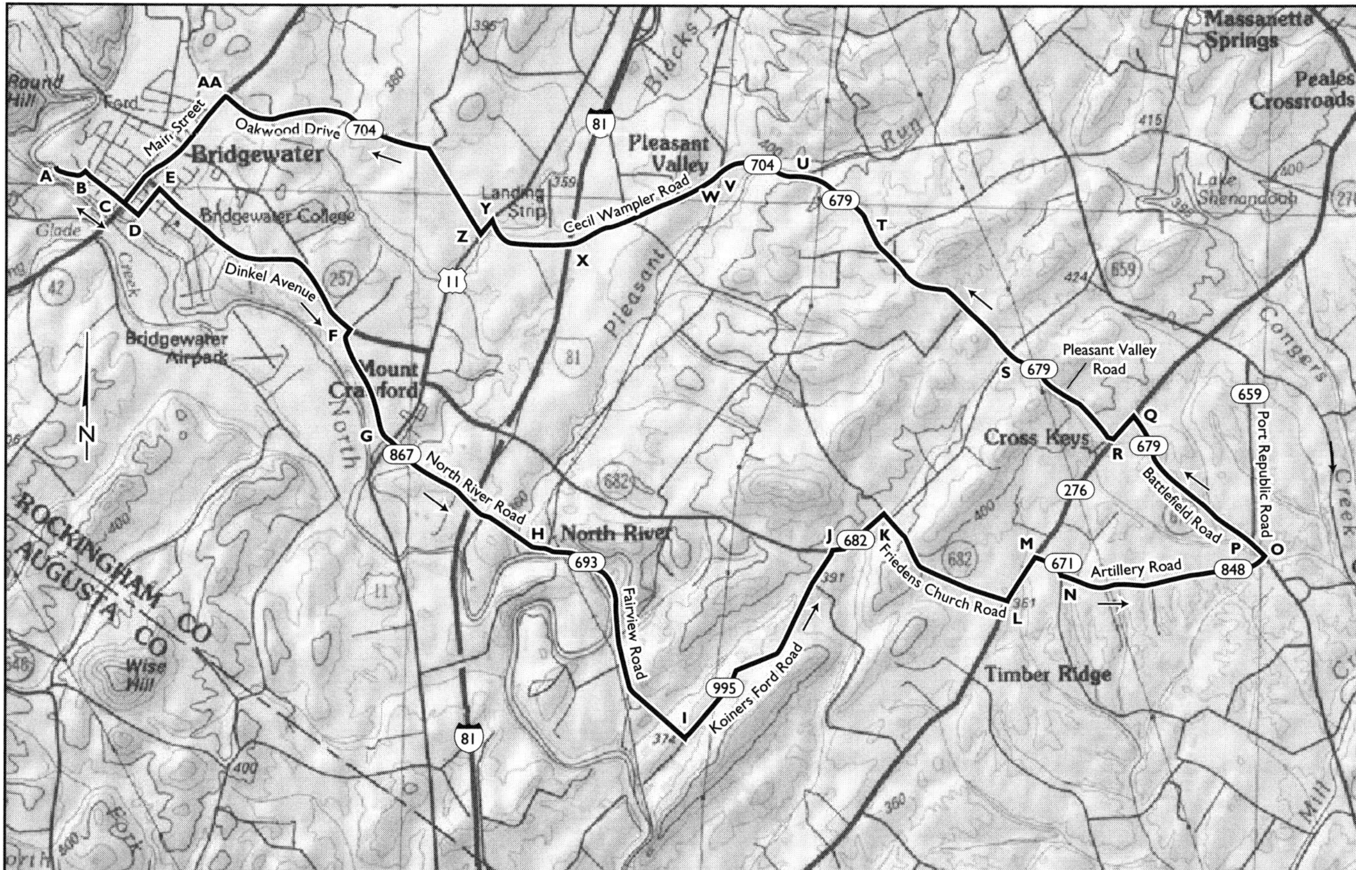

Massanetta Springs
Peales Crossroads
Round Hill
Ford
AA
Main Street
Oakwood Drive
704
81
Pleasant Valley
Bridgewater
A
B
C
D
E
Glade
Creek
Bridgewater College
Landing Strip
Y
Z
Cecil Wampler Road
W
V
704
U
679
T
X
Lake Shenandoah
Run
Dinkel Avenue
257
11
Pleasant
42
F
Bridgewater Airpark
Mount Crawford
81
659
Pleasant Valley Road
S
679
Congers
659
Port Republic Road
N
North
G
867
North River Road
Cross Keys
Q
R
679
Battlefield Road
276
682
H
North River
693
J
682
K
Friedens Church Road
682
M
671
Artillery Road
848
P
O
N
L
11
Fairview Road
Koiners Ford Road
995
I
Timber Ridge
ROCKINGHAM CO
AUGUSTA CO
Wise Hill
81
Mill
Creek

Ride 10: Bridgewater East

POINT	MILES	DESCRIPTION
N	11.3	Straight/bear left on Rt 848 Artillery Rd
O	13.0	Left on Rt 659 Port Republic Rd
P	13.1	Left on Rt 679 Battlefield Rd. Pass Civil War battlefield
Q	14.5	Left on Rt 276 Cross Keys Rd
R	14.8	Right on Rt 679 Pleasant Valley Rd
S	15.8	Cross Rt 680 Oak Ridge Rd
T	17.1	Cross Rt 689 Spaders Church Rd
U	17.9	Straight on Rt 704/679 Pleasant Valley Rd
V	18.5	Left on Rt 704 Cecil Wampler Rd
W	18.7	Cross railroad tracks
X	20.0	Cross I-81 (no interchange)
Y	20.7	Left on Rt 11 Valley Pike. Store here
Z	20.9	Right on Rt 704 Oakwood Dr
AA	23.3	Left on Rt 42 N Main St
C	24.3	Right on Bank St
B	24.7	Left on Bank St toward park
A	24.9	Finish at Wildwood Park

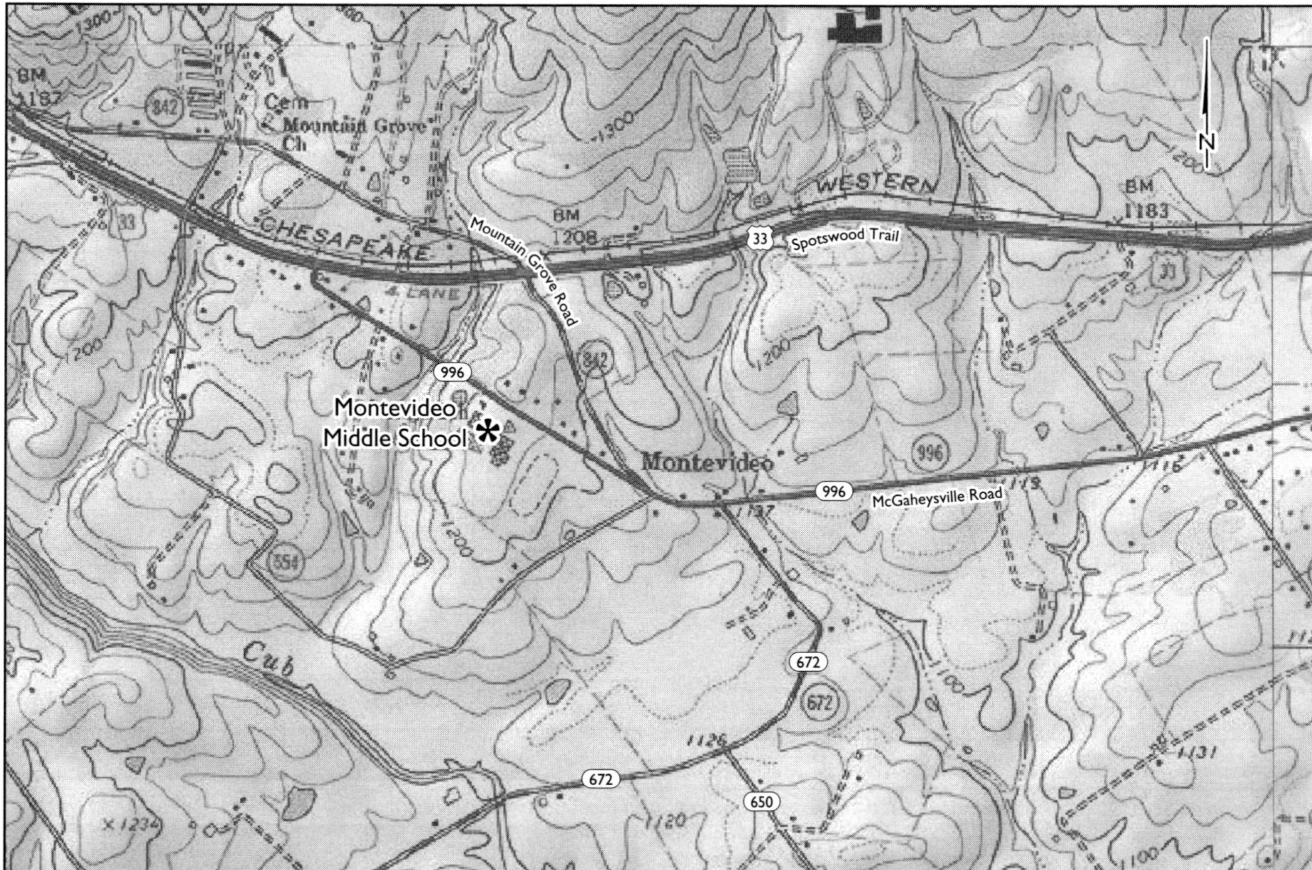
Montevideo
Middle School
Montevideo
McGaheysville Road
996
Spotswood Trail
33
Mountain Grove Road
842
CHESAPEAKE
WESTERN
4 LANE
Cem
Mountain Grove
Ch
BM
1187
BM
1208
BM
1183
554
672
650
Cub
N

Ride 11: Montevideo

Pineville, Port Republic, Grottoes, Goods Mill

This relatively flat ride explores the eastern part of Rockingham County and offers great views of the Blue Ridge Mountains. It is convenient for people visiting Massanutten Resort. A 12-mile option allows riders to do a shorter route.

DISTANCE 23.6 miles

ELEVATION CHANGE 680 feet

TRAFFIC LEVEL Low, but use caution on Route 659 Port Republic Road and Route 256 Weyers Cave Road, which are busier secondary roads.

TERRAIN Relatively flat for the first half, but more rolling after Grottoes.

STORES ALONG THE ROUTE Two, on Port Republic Road in Port Republic, and at the intersection of Route 256 and Route 825 Dogwood Avenue in Grottoes.

START LOCATION Montevideo Middle School. Montevideo Middle School is on the south side of Route 996 McGaheysville Road in Penn Laird, between Elkton and Harrisonburg. From Elkton, take Route 33 West and turn left on McGaheysville Road. From Harrisonburg, take Route 33 East and turn right on McGaheysville Road. A brown sign on Route 33 should indicate the turns.

COMMENTS This ride can be started from either Grottoes or Montevideo. If starting from Grottoes, do not follow Pineville Road all the way to Montevideo. Turn right onto Lawyer Road instead and resume directions. For an approximately 12-mile shortcut when doing the ride from Montevideo, turn right at Route 671 Doe Hill Road (point E), right again at Route 659 Port Republic Road, then right on Route 672 Pineville Road (point U) to rejoin the described route.

POINT	MILES	DESCRIPTION
A	0.0	Exit Montevideo Middle School turning right on Rt 996 McGaheysville Rd
B	0.4	Right on Rt 672 Pineville Rd
C	2.0	Left on Rt 655 Lawyer Rd
D	3.5	Bear right continuing on Rt 655 Lawyer Rd
E	6.7	Continue straight on Rt 655 Lawyer Rd. For shortcut, turn right on Rt 671 Doe Hill Rd
F	7.0	Left on Rt 659 Port Republic Rd
G	7.5	Continue straight. Store here
H	7.7	Right on Rt 825 South River Rd. Rt 825 South River Rd becomes Rt 825 Dogwood Ave in Grottoes

Montevideo
McGaheysville Road
996
672
Pineville Road
Pineville
Goods Mill
Lawyer Road
655
708
673
672
Port Republic Road
Longs Hill
Doe Hill Road
671
Mill Creek Church Road
668
828
659
Lynnwood
Port Republic
825
Timber Ridge Road
Lee Roy Road
Dogwood Avenue
Grottoes
Weyers Cave Road
256
Mt Meridian
Grand Caverns
Cross Keys
Timber Ridge
South Fork
Lewis Peak
Lewis Mountain
Austin Mountain
Madison
N

Ride 11: Montevideo

POINT	MILES	DESCRIPTION
I	10.1	Right on Rt 256 3rd St/Weyers Cave Rd. Store here
J	11.5	Right on Rt 605 Lee Roy Rd
K	12.6	Left on Rt 668 Timber Ridge Rd
L	14.5	Continue straight on Rt 668 Timber Ridge Rd
M	15.4	Continue straight on Rt 668 Timber Ridge Rd
N	16.1	Right on Rt 672 Mill Creek Church Rd. Wind around on Mill Creek Church Rd, staying on paved roads
O	17.3	Bear right on Rt 672 Mill Creek Church Rd
P	17.6	Left on Rt 673 Mill Creek Church Rd. Rt 672 turns right
Q	18.6	Left on Rt 659 Port Republic Rd.
R	18.9	Right on Rt 676 Charlie Town Rd
S	19.0	Right on Rt 676 Trimble Rd
T	19.4	Right on Rt 708/676 Goods Mill Rd
U	19.9	Left on Rt 672 Pineville Rd. Shortcut rejoins here
B	23.2	Left on Rt 996 McGaheysville Rd
A	23.6	Left to finish at Montevideo Middle School

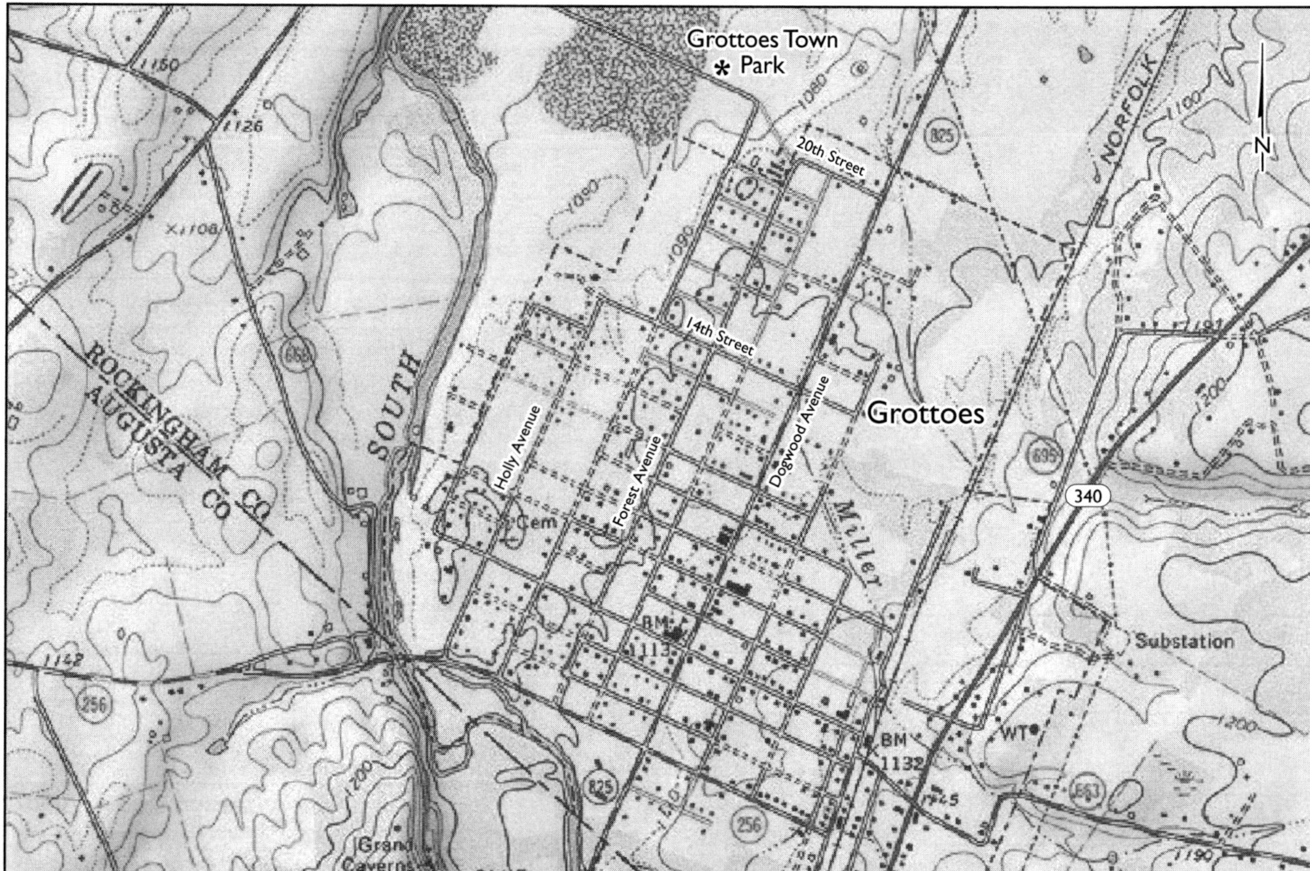
Grottoes Town
Park
20th Street
14th Street
Grottoes
Holly Avenue
Forest Avenue
Dogwood Avenue
Miller
SOUTH
ROCKINGHAM CO
AUGUSTA CO
NORFOLK
340
Substation
Grand
Caverns
N

Ride 12: Grottoes

Harriston, Piedmont, Mount Meridian

This unusually flat ride by Shenandoah Valley standards begins and ends in the quiet, bike-friendly town of Grottoes and travels through farmlands. Soon after leaving Grottoes, you pass the entrance to Cave Hill Park, site of Grand Caverns, a tourist attraction featuring natural limestone formations. After meandering along the South River, the route traverses rolling hills southwest of Grottoes. A shorter option takes approximately three miles off the route.

DISTANCE 16.9 miles

ELEVATION CHANGE 470 feet

TRAFFIC LEVEL Low, except when on or crossing Route 256 Weyers Cave Road and Route 825 Dogwood Avenue.

TERRAIN Very flat through Grottoes and along the South River, with only a few rolling hills from the middle to the end.

STORES ALONG THE ROUTE One, near the start at the intersection of Route 825 Dogwood Avenue and Route 256 Weyers Cave Road.

START LOCATION Grottoes Town Park. Grottoes is located at the junction of Routes 256 and 340. From the north or south take Route 340 from Elkton or Waynesboro respectively and turn west onto Route 256. From the west, take Route 256 East from I-81. Once on Route 256, turn north (the Blue Ridge Mountains will be on your right) on Route 825 Dogwood Avenue. Turn left on 20th Street, which ends at the park entrance.

COMMENTS This ride could be combined with the ride out of Montevideo to make a longer loop. Also, the Waynesboro North (long) route could be extended slightly to give riders a chance to stop at a store in Grottoes or add a few more miles. Riders wanting a shorter route can subtract 3.2 miles by turning right on Route 865 Rockfish Road instead of crossing it (point F), and following it to Route 256 Weyers Cave Road (point H).

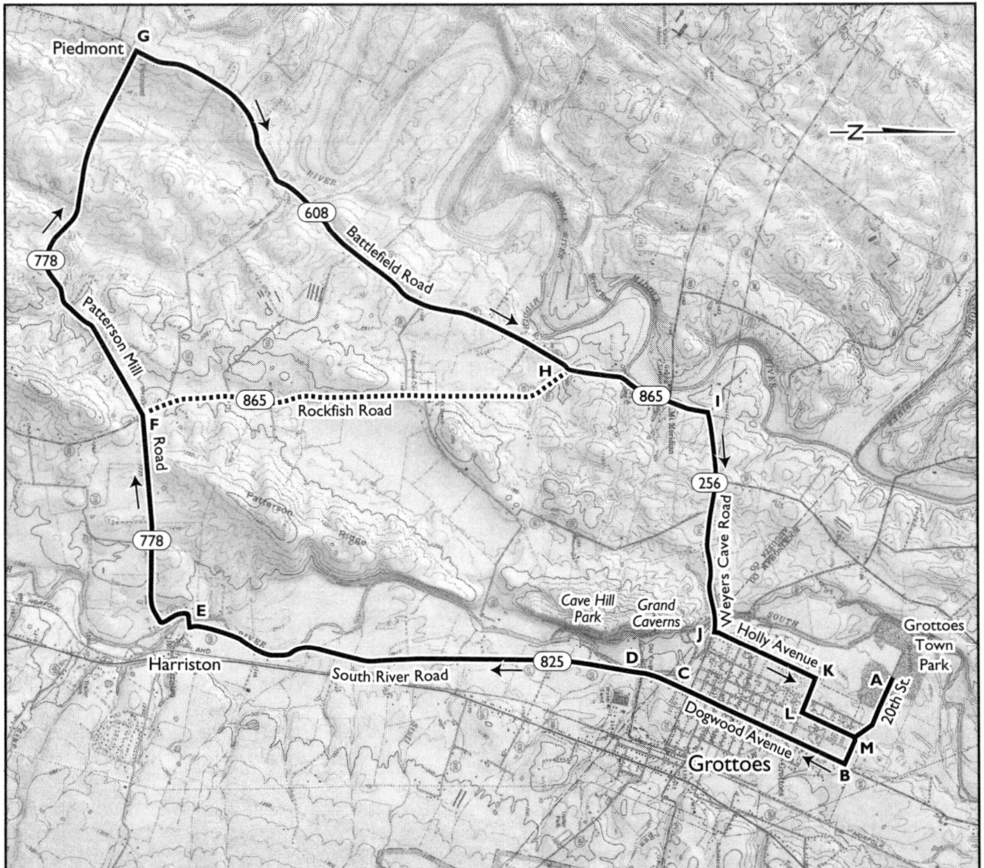
Piedmont
G
608
Battlefield Road
778
Patterson Mill
Road
F
865
Rockfish Road
H
865
I
256
Weyers Cave Road
778
Patterson Ridge
E
Cave Hill Park
Grand Caverns
J
Holly Avenue
K
Grottoes Town Park
A
20th St.
Harriston
825
South River Road
D
C
L
Dogwood Avenue
M
Grottoes
B
N

Ride 12: Grottoes

POINT	MILES	DESCRIPTION
A	0.0	Exit Grottoes Town Park turning left at the yield sign. This road becomes 20th St at Forest Ave crossing
B	0.7	Right on Rt 825 Dogwood Ave
C	1.8	Cross Rt 256. Rt 825 Dogwood Ave becomes Rt 825 South River Rd. Store here
D	2.1	Pass entrance to Cave Hill Park and Grand Caverns
E	5.1	Right on Rt 778 Patterson Mill Rd
F	6.5	Cross Rt 865 Rockfish Rd. Shortcut turns right here
G	9.1	Right on Rt 608 Battlefield Rd
H	12.7	Left on Rt 865 Rockfish Rd. Shortcut rejoins here
I	13.8	Right on Rt 256 Weyers Cave Rd
J	15.1	Left on Holly Ave
K	15.8	Right on 14th St
L	16.0	Left on Forest Ave
M	16.4	Left on 20th St
A	16.9	Finish at Grottoes Town Park

Augusta County

rides leaving from

Staunton

Fort Defiance

Craigsville

Waynesboro

Stuarts Draft

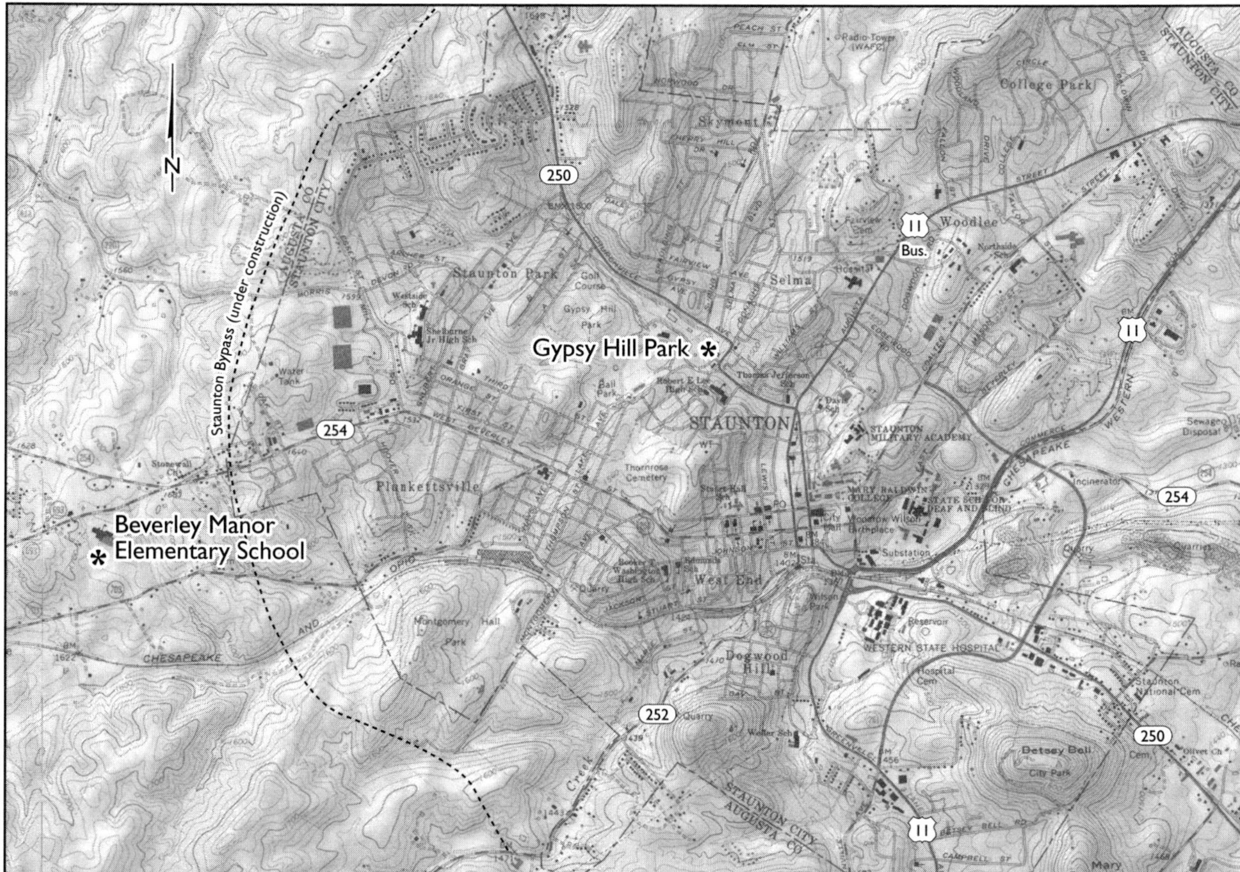
N
Gypsy Hill Park
Beverley Manor
Elementary School
Staunton Bypass (under construction)
STAUNTON
250
254
252
11
11
Bus.

Ride 13: Staunton Northeast

Quicks Mill, Mount Pisgah, Roman, Spring Hill

Despite always being within a handful of miles of I-81, this ride seems much more remote because the hilly terrain keeps it well hidden. The trek along the one-lane, little-traveled Route 732 Roman Road through quiet farm country makes you feel like you are really getting away. The very twisty Route 626 Limestone Road also is never boring. Riders wishing to shorten the route may chose an approximately 19.5-mile option.

DISTANCE 25.7 miles

ELEVATION CHANGE 1,860 feet

TRAFFIC LEVEL Moderate. Use caution on Route 613 Spring Hill Road heading in and out of Staunton and when on or crossing Route 275 Staunton Bypass and Route 250 Churchville Road.

TERRAIN Hilly.

STORES ALONG THE ROUTE None.

START LOCATION Gypsy Hill Park. Exit I-81 for Route 250 (exit 222) to Staunton. Follow Route 250 West as it winds around and makes several turns at major intersections. Pay careful attention to the Route 250 signs. Just before the park entrance, which will be on the left, there is a large old school complex. The sign at the park entrance is small and easy to miss.

COMMENTS Riders can take a shortcut for an approximately 19.5-mile route. Turn left on Route 742 Mount Pisgah Road instead of crossing it (point G). Continue straight as Mount Pisgah Road changes from Route 742 to Route 745. Turn left on Route 745 Todd Road and left again on Route 732 Roman Road to rejoin the ride (between points J and K). This route overlaps briefly with the Fort Defiance North route, so it can be extended if desired.

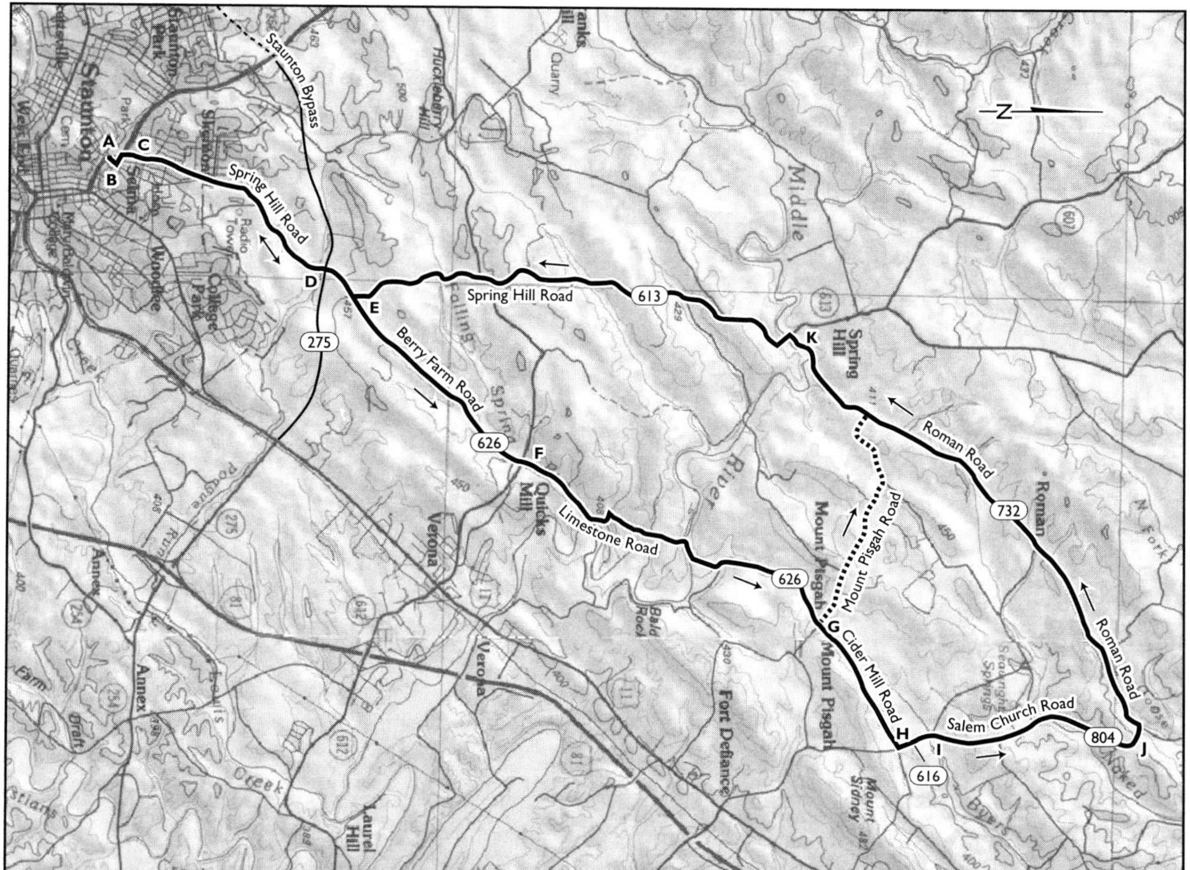

Staunton
Staunton Park
Staunton Bypass
A
B
C
D
E
F
G
H
I
J
K
Spring Hill Road
Radio Tower
Woodlee
College Park
West End
Mary Baldwin College
275
Huckleberry Hill
Quarry
Middle
N
Spring Hill
613
607
Berry Farm Road
Falling Spring
626
Quicks Mill
Verona
Limestone Road
River
Mount Pisgah Road
Mount Pisgah
Roman Road
Roman
732
Cider Mill Road
Bald Rock
Fort Defiance
Salem Church Road
804
616
Mount Sidney
Laurel Hill
Annex
Naked Creek
Byers
Christians Creek

Ride 13: Staunton Northeast

POINT	MILES	DESCRIPTION
A	0.0	Exit Gypsy Hill Park main entrance and turn left on Rt 250 Churchville Rd
B	0.1	Left on Rt 250 Churchville Rd at light
C	0.2	Right on Rt 613 Spring Hill Rd
D	2.5	Cross Rt 275 Staunton Bypass
E	2.9	Continue straight. Rt 613 Spring Hill Rd becomes Rt 626 Berry Farm Rd
F	5.2	Cross Rt 612 Quicks Mill Rd. Rt 626 Berry Farm Rd becomes Rt 626 Limestone Rd
G	8.7	Cross Rt 742 Mt Pisgah Rd. Rt 626 Limestone Rd becomes Rt 626 Cider Mill Rd. Shortcut turns left here
H	10.2	Left on Rt 616 Salem Church Rd
I	10.5	Bear right on Rt 804 Salem Church Rd
J	12.8	Left on Rt 732 Roman Rd. Shortcut rejoins about three-quarters of the way to the next intersection
K	18.0	Left on Rt 613 Spring Hill Rd
E	22.8	Right on Rt 613 Spring Hill Rd
D	23.1	Cross Rt 275 Staunton Bypass
C	25.5	Left on Rt 250 Churchville Rd
B	25.6	Right on Rt 250 Churchville Rd at light
A	25.7	Right into Gypsy Hill Park main entrance to finish

Ride 14: Staunton North (short)

Franks Mill, Spring Hill

This lollipop-shaped loop heads north from Staunton into lovely farm country. Route 732 Middle River Road is narrow and relatively untraveled. On the way back, Route 742 Shutterlee Mill Road follows a ridge and offers delightful views of the mountains in all directions.

DISTANCE 19.6 miles

ELEVATION CHANGE 1,210 feet

TRAFFIC LEVEL Moderate. Use caution on Route 613 heading in and out of Staunton and while on or crossing Route 275 Staunton Bypass and Route 250 Churchville Road.

TERRAIN Hilly, with climbing spread throughout the ride.

STORES ALONG THE ROUTE None.

START LOCATION Gypsy Hill Park. Exit I-81 for Route 250 (exit 222) to Staunton. Follow Route 250 West as it winds around and makes several turns at major intersections. Pay careful attention to the Route 250 signs. Just before the park entrance, which will be on the left, there is a large old school complex. The sign at the park entrance is small and easy to miss.

COMMENTS Shutterlee Road is a winding road with many turnoffs. When in doubt at intersections, stay on Shutterlee Road unless the directions indicate otherwise. You will do a substantial amount of climbing on Shutterlee Road (both sections) and Middle River Road. Riders wanting to return to Staunton a different way should stay on Route 613 Spring Hill Road out of Spring Hill and follow directions from the Staunton Northeast ride (point K on that route) back to Gypsy Hill Park.

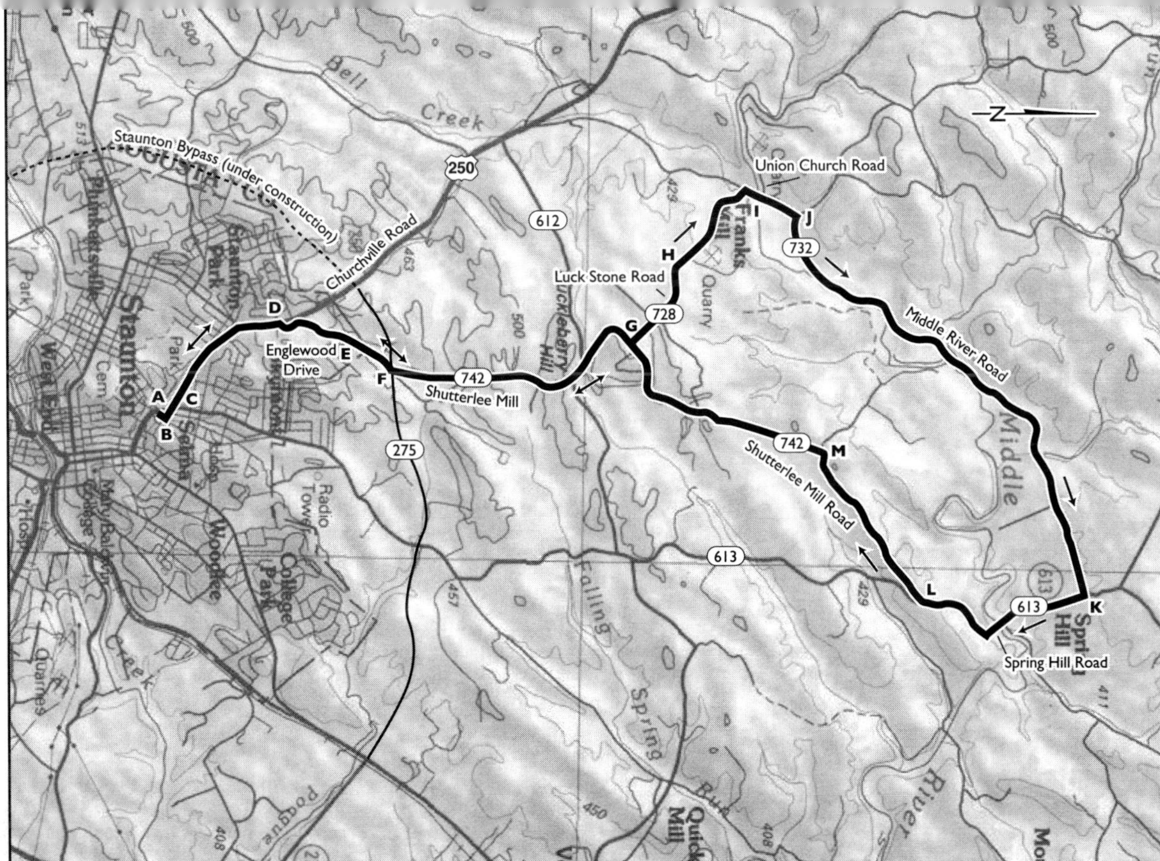

STAUNTON NORTH (SHORT)

Ride 14: Staunton North (short)

POINT	MILES	DESCRIPTION
A	0.0	Exit Gypsy Hill Park main entrance and turn left on Rt 250 Churchville Rd
B	0.1	Left on Rt 250 Churchville Rd at light
C	0.2	Continue straight on Rt 250 Churchville Rd
D	1.3	Right on Englewood Dr
E	2.1	Continue straight. Englewood Dr becomes Rt 742 Shutterlee Mill Rd
F	2.4	Cross Rt 275 Staunton Bypass. Continue on Rt 742 Shutterlee Rd as it winds around
G	4.4	Left on Rt 728 Luck Stone Rd
H	5.2	Pass quarry entrance
I	5.9	Right on Rt 732/728 Union Church Rd
J	6.4	Bear right on Rt 732 Middle River Rd
K	10.4	Right on Rt 613 Spring Hill Rd
L	11.9	Right on Rt 742 Shutterlee Mill Rd
M	13.3	Bear left on Rt 742 Shutterlee Mill Rd
G	15.1	Straight on Rt 742 Shutterlee Mill Rd
F	17.1	Cross Rt 275 Staunton Bypass
E	17.9	Continue straight. Rt 742 Shutterlee Mill Rd becomes Rt 742 Englewood Rd
D	18.2	Left on Rt 250 Churchville Rd
C	19.4	Straight on Rt 250 Churchville Rd
B	19.5	Right on Rt 250 Churchville Rd at light
A	19.6	Right into Gypsy Hill Park main entrance to finish

Ride 15: Staunton North (long)

Spring Hill, Moscow, Mount Solon, Parnassus, Franks Mill

This scenic ride offers frequent and wonderful views of the Blue Ridge Mountains and the Shenandoah, Great North, and Narrowback Mountains. It is very hilly, but the beautiful route takes advantage of some of the area's finest rural roads. Riders looking for a diversion may wish to visit Natural Chimneys as a side trip along the way.

DISTANCE 34.6 miles

ELEVATION CHANGE 2,580 feet

TRAFFIC LEVEL Low overall, but use caution heading in and out of Staunton and when on or crossing Route 275 Staunton Bypass and Route 42 Scenic Highway.

TERRAIN Very hilly, with many tough climbs in the second half.

STORES ALONG THE ROUTE One, less than halfway at the intersection of Route 747 Free Mason Run Road and Route 731 Natural Chimneys Road in Mount Solon.

START LOCATION Gypsy Hill Park. Exit I-81 for Route 250 (exit 222) to Staunton. Follow Route 250 West as it winds around and makes several turns at major intersections. Pay careful attention to the Route 250 signs. Just before the park entrance, which will be on the left, there is a large old school complex. The sign at the park entrance is small and easy to miss.

COMMENTS Use this ride to connect with routes heading southwest from Bridgewater. Riders wishing to visit Natural Chimneys should continue straight on Route 731 Natural Chimneys Road instead of turning left on Route 747 Free Mason Run Road (point K). This ride is not suitable for beginners or those who tire easily on hills, but it can be very rewarding for more experienced riders.

POINT	MILES	DESCRIPTION
A	0.0	Exit Gypsy Hill Park main entrance and turn left on Rt 250 Churchville Rd
B	0.1	Left on Rt 250 Churchville Rd at light
C	0.2	Right on Rt 613 Spring Hill Rd
D	2.5	Cross Rt 275 Staunton Bypass
E	2.9	Left on Rt 613 Spring Hill Rd
F	7.7	Straight on Rt 613 Spring Hill Rd near bridge
G	8.3	Straight on Rt 613 Spring Hill Rd
H	8.6	Bear left on Rt 607 Mt Solon Rd
I	13.3	Cross Rt 42 Scenic Hwy

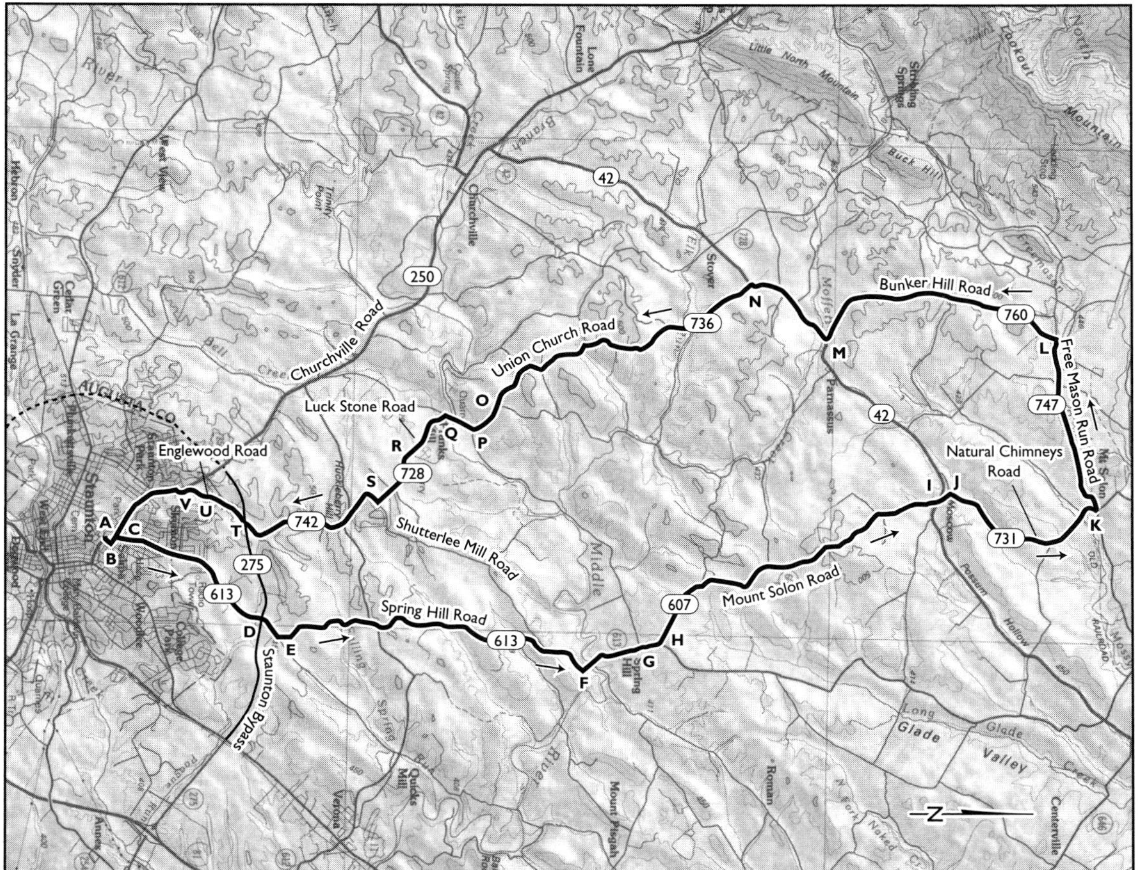
Staunton
Churchville Road
Union Church Road
Luck Stone Road
Englewood Road
Shutterlee Mill Road
Spring Hill Road
Mount Solon Road
Bunker Hill Road
Free Mason Run Road
Natural Chimneys Road
Staunton Bypass
250
42
736
728
742
275
613
607
760
747
731
A
B
C
D
E
F
G
H
I
J
K
L
M
N
O
P
Q
R
S
T
U
V
Churchville
Lone Fountain
Little North Mountain
North Mountain
Lookout
Buck Hill
Stribling Springs
Stover
Moffett
Parnassus
Middle
Trinity Point
West View
Hebron
Snyder
La Grange
Cedar Green
Mount Pisgah
Roman
Quicks Mill
Verona
Spring Hill
Long Glade
Glade Valley
Creek
Centerville
Moscow
Possum Hollow
Mt Solon
River
Z

Ride 15: Staunton North (long)

POINT	MILES	DESCRIPTION
J	13.5	Bear right on Rt 731 Natural Chimneys Rd
K	16.0	Left on Rt 747 Free Mason Run Rd. Store here
L	18.4	Left on Rt 760 Bunker Hill Rd
M	22.0	Right on Rt 42 Scenic Hwy
N	23.4	Left on Rt 736 Union Church Rd. Road is hilly and twisty, with many intersecting roads. Stay on Union Church Rd over next five miles
O	27.7	Straight on Rt 736 Union Church Rd
P	28.1	Bear right on Rt 732/728 Union Church Rd
Q	28.5	Left on Rt 728 Luck Stone Rd
R	29.3	Pass quarry entrance
S	30.1	Right on Rt 742 Shutterlee Mill Rd
T	32.1	Cross Rt 275 Staunton Bypass
U	32.9	Continue straight. Rt 742 Shutterlee Mill Rd becomes Rt 742 Englewood Rd
V	33.2	Left on Rt 250 Churchville Rd
C	34.4	Straight on Rt 250 Churchville Rd
B	34.5	Right on Rt 250 Churchville Rd at light
A	34.6	Right into Gypsy Hill Park main entrance to finish

Ride 16: Staunton West

Cedar Green, Swoope, Trimbles Mill, Hebron

Ride quiet roads with beautiful scenery, including spectacular views of Elliot Knob—a high point along the imposing Great North Mountain—and surrounding areas of George Washington National Forest. You also will pass near the Trimble Mountain Boy Scout camp. Riders wanting a shorter route can choose an approximately 15-mile option.

DISTANCE 20.9 miles

ELEVATION CHANGE 1,325 feet

TRAFFIC LEVEL Low, but use caution when on or crossing Route 254 Parkersburg Turnpike.

TERRAIN Rolling, with climbing and descending spread evenly throughout.

STORES ALONG THE ROUTE None.

START LOCATION Beverley Manor Elementary School. From downtown Staunton, take Route 254 West to the Staunton city/Augusta County border. Cross under Route 262 Staunton Bypass (under construction at press time). Turn left on Route 693 Cedar Green Road. Turn left into Beverley Manor Elementary School.

COMMENTS For an approximately 15-mile loop, turn left at Route 703 Hewitt Road (point H). Stay on this road as it twists and turns through farmlands until it gets to Hebron, where continuing straight on Route 703 Hebron Road (point R) will connect you to the rest of the loop.

STAUNTON WEST

Ride 16: Staunton West

POINT	MILES	DESCRIPTION
A	0.0	Exit Beverley Manor Elementary School turning left on Rt 693 Cedar Green Rd
B	0.8	Right on Rt 704 William Cousins Rd
C	1.5	Left on Rt 254 Parkersburg Turnpike
D	1.7	Right on Rt 612 Frog Pond Rd
E	2.8	Left on Rt 720 Morris Mill Rd
F	7.0	Left on Rt 833 Trinity Point Rd
G	8.3	Right on Rt 254 Parkersburg Turnpike
—	8.4	Left on Rt 876 Swoope Rd
H	10.0	Right on Rt 703 Hewitt Rd. Shortcut goes left here
I	10.7	Left on Rt 876 Cattleman Rd
J	11.9	Right on Rt 876/707 Cattleman Rd
K	12.5	Right on Rt 707 Trimbles Mill Rd
L	13.3	Bear left on Rt 705 Trimbles Mill Rd. North Mountain Rd joins from the right

POINT	MILES	DESCRIPTION
M	13.5	Bear left on Rt 707 Trimbles Mill Rd. Boy Scout Camp Rd joins from the right
N	14.6	Left on Rt 876 Glebe School Rd
O	14.9	Straight on Rt 708 Glebe School Rd
P	17.2	Bear left on Rt 708 Glebe School Rd
Q	17.8	Left on Rt 708 Eidson Creek Rd
R	18.4	Right on Rt 703 Hebron Rd. Shortcut rejoins here
S	19.5	Left on Rt 693 Cedar Green Rd
—	19.6	Right on Rt 703 Buttermilk Springs Rd after crossing bridge
T	20.4	Left into Beverley Manor Middle School
A	20.9	Finish at Beverley Manor Elementary School

Ride 17: Staunton Southwest

Cedar Green, Hebron, Arbor Hill, Middlebrook, Trimbles Mill

If you enjoy visiting rural places and imagining what life must have been like 50 or 100 years ago, this ride through farmlands is for you. A section of the ride takes you on a one-lane paved farm road. The entire route provides opportunities to enjoy views of the mountains and quiet, sparsely populated valleys.

DISTANCE 25.1 miles

ELEVATION CHANGE 1,385 feet

TRAFFIC LEVEL Low, but use caution when on or crossing Route 252 Middlebrook Road and Route 693 Cedar Green Road, which may have heavier traffic.

TERRAIN Rolling. The climbing occurs predominantly in the first half, while most of the descending occurs in the second half.

STORES ALONG THE ROUTE None.

START LOCATION Beverley Manor Elementary School. From downtown Staunton, take Route 254 West to the Staunton city/Augusta County border. Cross under Route 262 Staunton Bypass (under construction at press time). Turn left on Route 693 Cedar Green Road. Turn left into Beverley Manor Elementary School.

COMMENTS This route can be enjoyed in either direction. For a really long, hilly ride more suitable for experts, it can be combined with the Staunton West route. For example, start riding on Staunton West, and at Glebe School Road join this route in reverse. Or, when you get to Glebe School Road doing this ride, start following the Staunton West ride in reverse.

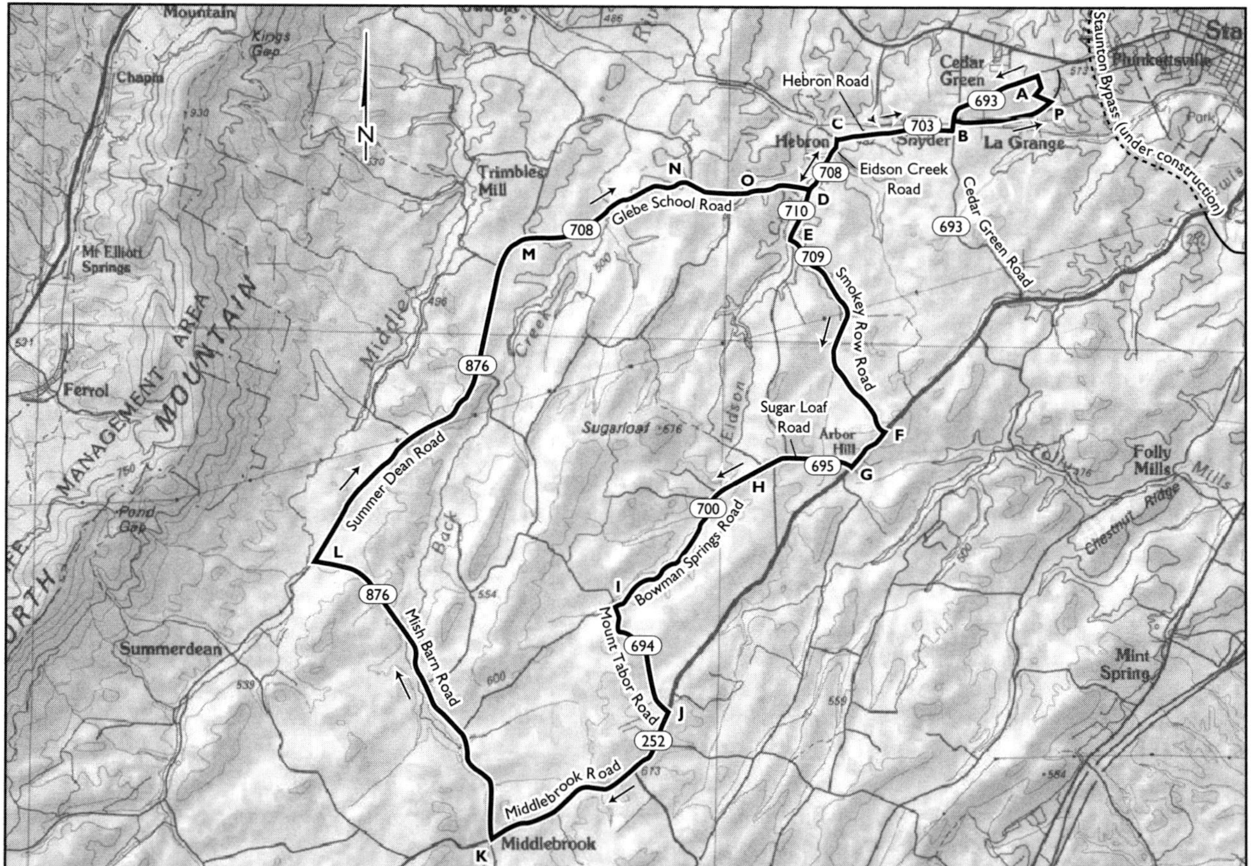

Mountain
Kings Gap
Chapin
N
Trimbles Mill
Cedar Green
Hebron Road
Hebron
Snyder
La Grange
Staunton Bypass (under construction)
Eidson Creek Road
Cedar Green Road
Glebe School Road
Mt Elliott Springs
MOUNTAIN
MANAGEMENT AREA
Middle
Creek
Ferrol
Smokey Row Road
Sugar Loaf Road
Arbor Hill
Sugarloaf
Eidson
Summer Dean Road
Pond Gap
Back
Folly Mills
Chestnut Ridge
Bowman Springs Road
Mount Tabor Road
Mish Barn Road
Summerdean
Mint Spring
Middlebrook Road
Middlebrook
693
703
708
710
709
695
700
694
252
876
A
B
C
D
E
F
G
H
I
J
K
L
M
N
O
P

Ride 17: Staunton Southwest

POINT	MILES	DESCRIPTION
A	0.0	Exit Beverley Manor Elementary School turning left on Rt 693 Cedar Green Rd
B	1.0	Right on Rt 703 Hebron Rd after crossing bridge
C	2.1	Left on Rt 708 Eidson Creek Rd
D	2.7	Bear left on Rt 710 Eidson Creek Rd
E	3.2	Continue straight on Rt 709 Smokey Row Rd
F	5.4	Right on Rt 252 Middlebrook Rd
G	5.9	Right on Rt 695 Sugar Loaf Rd
H	7.3	Bear left on Rt 700 Bowman Springs Rd
I	8.8	Left on Rt 694 Mt Tabor Rd
J	9.9	Right on Rt 252 Middlebrook Rd
K	12.1	Right on Rt 876 Mish Barn Rd
L	15.4	Right on Rt 876 Summer Dean Rd (becomes Glebe School Rd)
M	19.2	Straight on Rt 708 Glebe School Rd
N	20.9	Straight on Rt 708 Glebe School Rd
O	21.4	Bear left on Rt 708 Glebe School Rd
D	22.0	Left on Rt 708 Eidson Creek Rd
C	22.6	Right on Rt 703 Hebron Rd
B	23.7	Left on Rt 693 Cedar Green Rd
—	23.8	Right on Rt 703 Buttermilk Springs Rd after crossing bridge
P	24.6	Left into Beverley Manor Middle School
A	25.1	Finish at Beverley Manor Elementary School

Ride 18: Staunton South

Cedar Green, Folly Mills

Tour southern Augusta County on this lollipop-shaped route. You will ride along a small ridge that runs from southwest to northeast, enjoying views of mountains to the east and west all along the way. And who can resist the chance to ride a road with the name of Stingy Hollow?

DISTANCE 20.0 miles

ELEVATION CHANGE 1,175 feet

TRAFFIC LEVEL Low to moderate. Use caution when on or crossing Route 693 Cedar Green Road and Route 252 Middlebrook Road.

TERRAIN Hilly. The high point occurs near the middle, but expect climbing and descending throughout the ride.

STORES ALONG THE ROUTE None.

START LOCATION Beverley Manor Elementary School. From downtown Staunton, take Route 254 West to the Staunton city/Augusta County border. Cross under Route 262 Staunton Bypass (under construction at press time). Turn left on Route 693 Cedar Green Road. Turn left into Beverley Manor Elementary School.

COMMENTS This ride is enjoyable in either direction, but the climbing is more sustained in the direction opposite from that described here. Riders starting on the south side of Staunton may wish to access this route at point H by heading south from town on Route 613 Old Greenville Road instead of first traveling to Beverley Manor Elementary School.

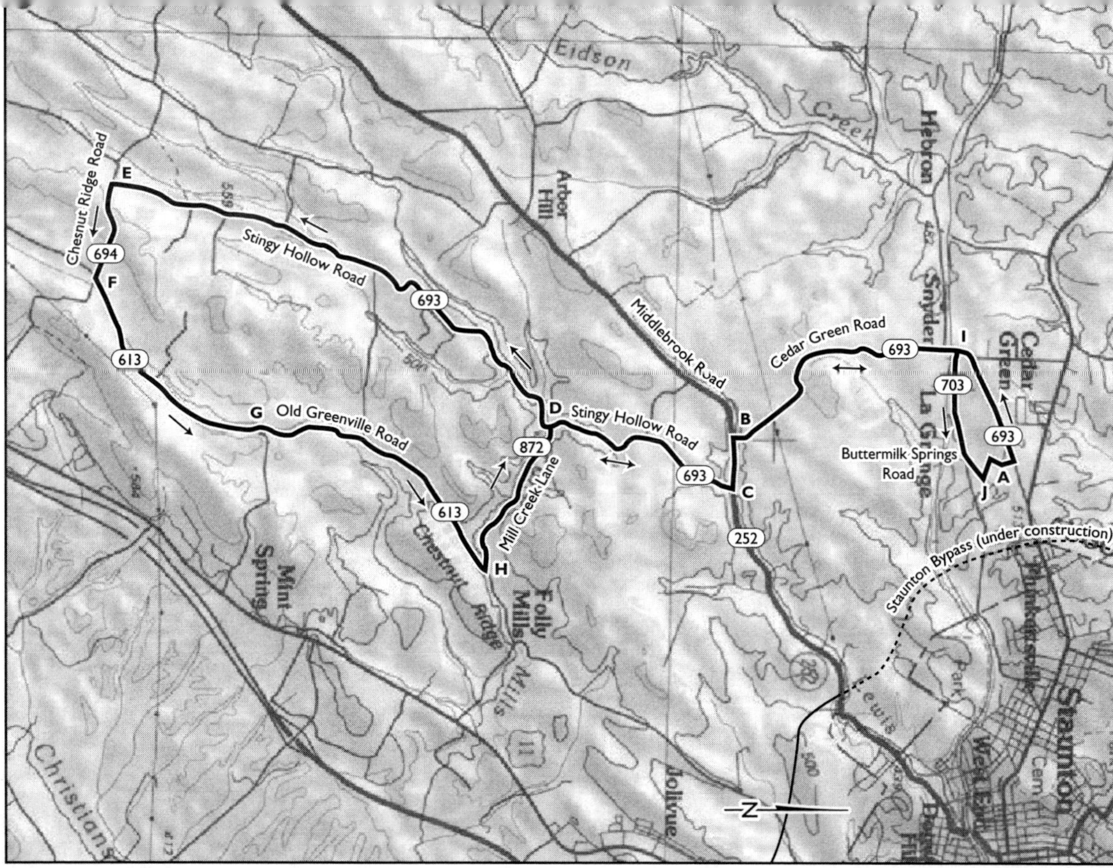

STAUNTON SOUTH

Ride 18: Staunton South

POINT	MILES	DESCRIPTION
A	0.0	Exit Beverley Manor School Elementary School turning left on Rt 693 Cedar Green Rd
B	3.0	Left on Rt 252 Middlebrook Rd
C	3.4	Right on Rt 693 Stingy Hollow Rd
D	4.9	Straight on Rt 693 Stingy Hollow Rd
E	8.9	Left on Rt 694 Chesnut Ridge Rd
F	9.6	Left on Rt 613 Old Greenville Rd
G	11.3	Bear left on Rt 613 Old Greenville Rd
H	13.5	Sharp left after bridge on Rt 872 Mill Creek Ln
D	14.7	Right on Rt 693 Stingy Hollow Rd
C	16.2	Left on Rt 252 Middlebrook Rd
B	16.6	Right on Rt 693 Cedar Green Rd
I	18.7	Right on Rt 703 Buttermilk Springs Rd
J	19.5	Left into Beverley Manor Middle School
A	20.0	Finish at Beverley Manor Elementary School

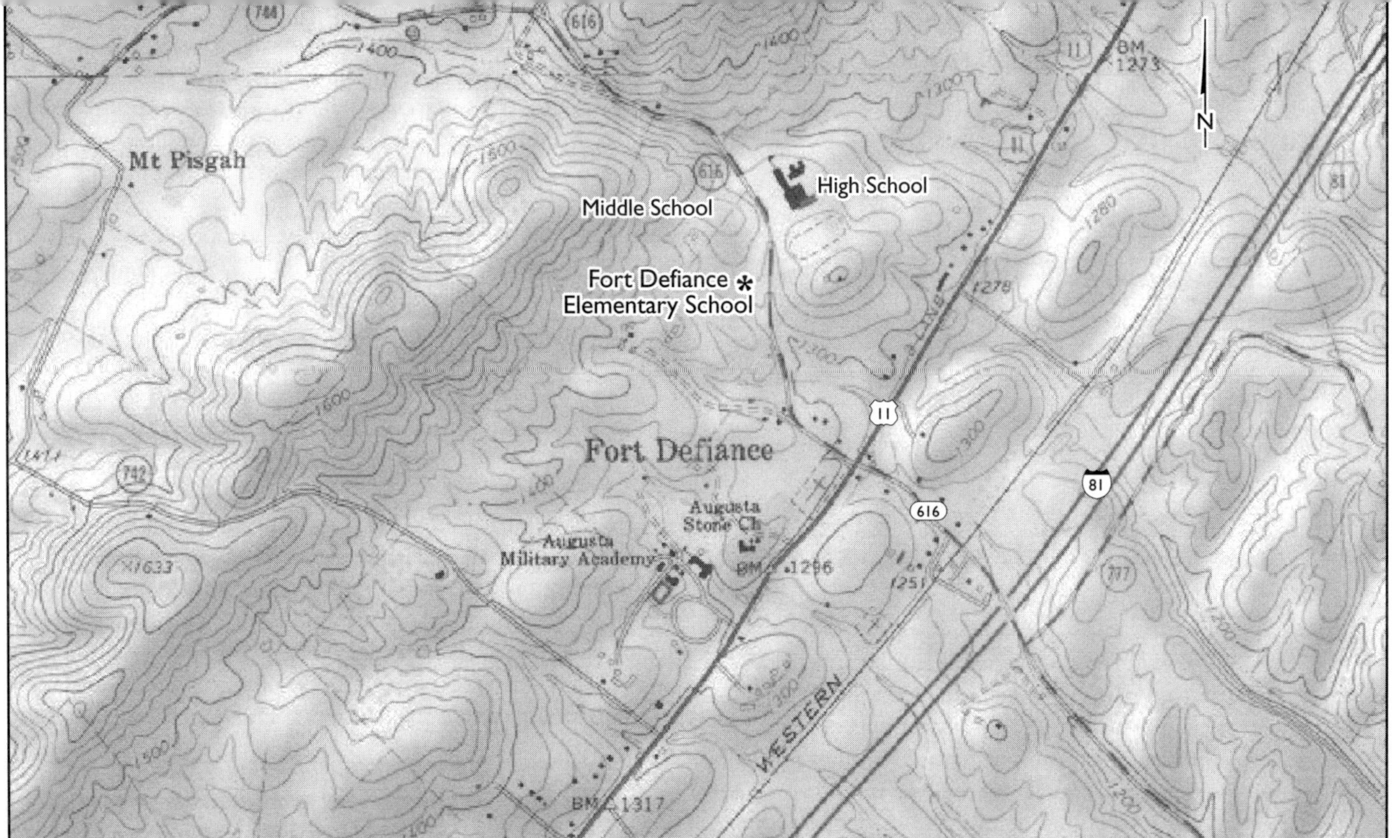

FORT DEFIANCE AREA

Ride 19: Fort Defiance North

Damtown, New Hope, Piedmont, Knightly, Mount Sidney

Enjoy quiet and scenic rural roads through central Augusta County. Cross the meandering Middle River twice, once at Damtown and once at Knightly, where the road traverses an old metal truss bridge with a wooden plank deck. Near the end, climb to the ride's highest point by Mount Sidney before the final descent into Fort Defiance. If you have time for only one ride in the area, this is it.

DISTANCE 15.9 miles

ELEVATION CHANGE 670 feet

TRAFFIC LEVEL Very low, except when on or crossing Route 11 Lee Highway.

TERRAIN Rolling.

STORES ALONG THE ROUTE One, at the intersection of Route 11 Lee Highway and Route 778 Knightly Mill Road in Mount Sidney.

START LOCATION Fort Defiance School Complex (Clymore Elementary School and Stewart Middle School). Fort Defiance High School is across the road. From I-81, exit at Verona (exit 227). Travel west on Route 612 Quicks Mill Road toward Verona. Turn right on Route 11 North. At Fort Defiance traffic light, turn left onto Route 616 Fort Defiance Road. Park at the elementary or middle school.

COMMENTS This ride can be combined with the Fort Defiance South ride for an approximately 25-mile route. Do the south loop first, and instead of turning back toward Fort Defiance on Route 616 Dam Town Road (point J on that route), continue on Route 608 Battlefield Road (point E on this route) and follow directions.

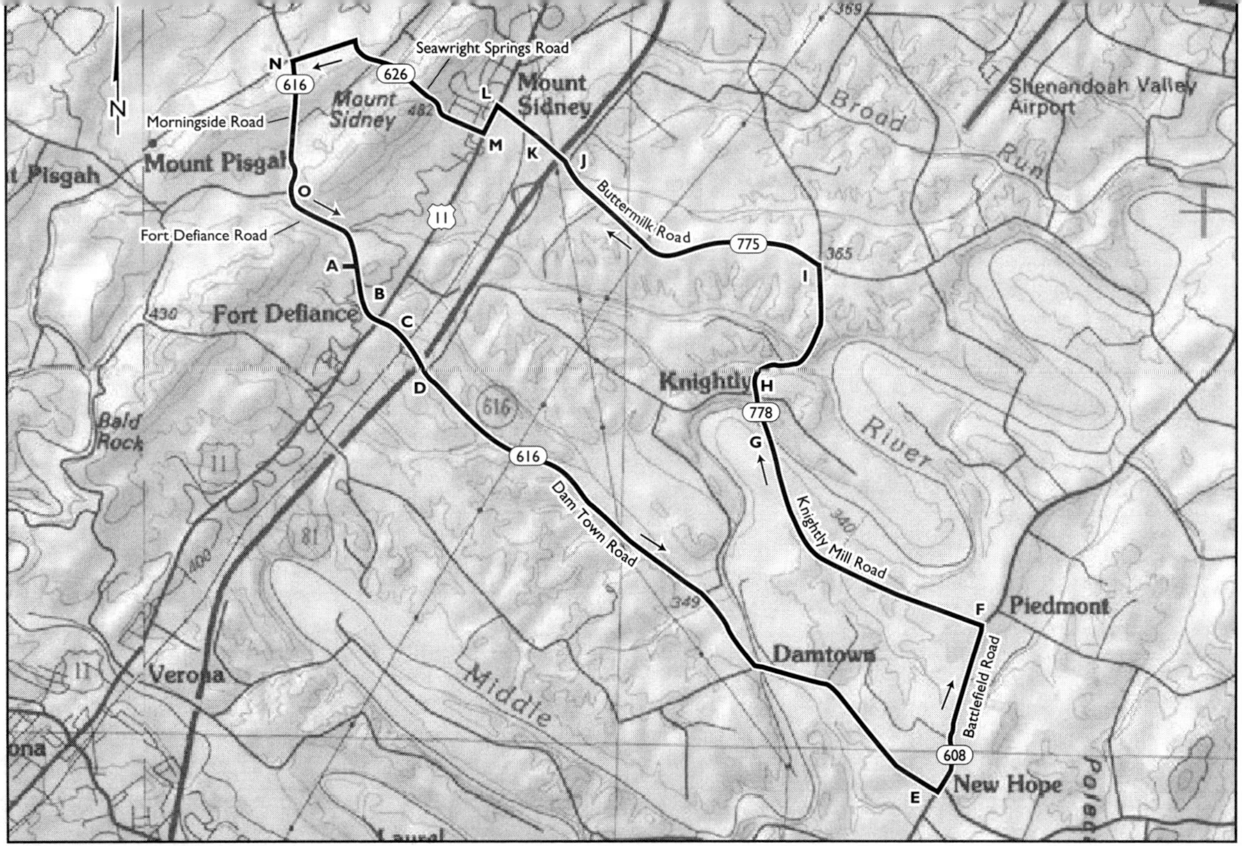

FORT DEFIANCE NORTH

Ride 19: Fort Defiance North

POINT	MILES	DESCRIPTION
A	0.0	Exit Ft Defiance School Complex (elementary or middle school) and turn right onto Rt 616 Ft Defiance Rd heading toward Rt 11
B	0.4	Cross Rt 11. Ft Defiance Rd becomes Rt 616 Dam Town Rd
C	0.7	Cross railroad tracks
D	0.8	Cross I-81 (no interchange)
E	5.4	Left on Rt 608 Battlefield Rd
F	6.6	Left on Rt 778 Knightly Mill Rd
G	8.7	Cross metal truss bridge with wood planks
H	8.9	Continue straight on Rt 778 Knightly Mill Rd. Rt 777 intersects
I	10.1	Left on Rt 775 Buttermilk Rd
J	12.1	Cross I-81 (no interchange)
K	12.4	Cross railroad tracks
L	12.6	Left on Rt 11 Lee Hwy. Store on left
M	12.8	Right on Rt 626 Seawright Springs Rd
N	14.4	Left on Rt 616 Morningside Rd
O	15.3	Left on Rt 616 Ft Defiance Rd
A	15.9	Finish at Ft Defiance School Complex

Ride 20: Fort Defiance South

Mount Pisgah, Quicks Mill, Verona, New Hope, Damtown

Ride through the heart of Augusta County on roads ranging from the narrow, twisty, wooded variety through Quicks Mill to more open farm country near New Hope, with good views of the Blue Ridge Mountains to the east.

DISTANCE 20.2 miles

ELEVATION CHANGE 930 feet

TRAFFIC LEVEL High on Route 612 Laurel Hill Road through Verona near I-81 and Route 11 intersections; low levels everywhere else.

TERRAIN Rolling.

STORES ALONG THE ROUTE Several on Route 612 Laurel Hill Road near I-81, and a small store at the New Hope intersection of Route 612 Laurel Hill Road and Route 608 Battlefield Road.

START LOCATION Fort Defiance School Complex (Clymore Elementary School and Stewart Middle School). Fort Defiance High School is across the road. From I-81, exit at Verona (exit 227). Travel west on Route 612 Quicks Mill Road toward Verona. Turn right on Route 11 North. At Fort Defiance traffic light, turn left onto Route 616 Fort Defiance Road. Park at the elementary or middle school.

COMMENTS This ride can be combined with the Fort Defiance North ride for an approximately 25-mile route. Do this loop first, and instead of turning back toward Fort Defiance on Route 616 Dam Town Road (point J on this route), continue straight on 608 Battlefield Road and follow directions from this intersection on the Fort Defiance North ride (point E on that route).

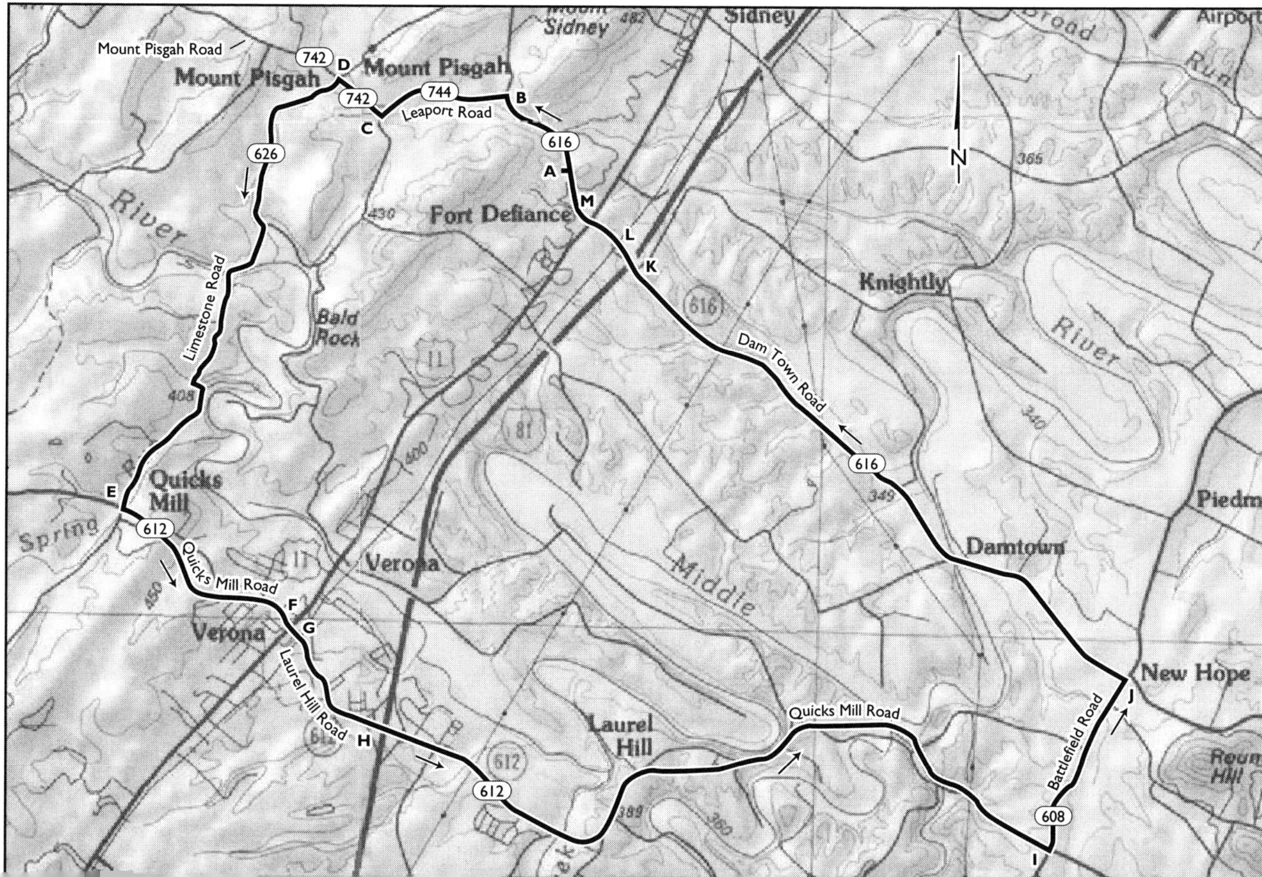

Mount Pisgah Road
742
D
Mount Pisgah
Mount Pisgah
742
744
Leaport Road
B
C
616
626
A
M
Fort Defiance
River
L
K
Knightly
616
Limestone Road
Bald Rock
Dam Town Road
River
408
616
E
Quicks Mill
612
Spring
Quicks Mill Road
Verona
F
G
Verona
Middle
Damtown
Piedmo
Laurel Hill Road
New Hope
J
Battlefield Road
Quicks Mill Road
Laurel Hill
H
612
612
608
I
Sidney
Airport
Round Hill
N

Ride 20: Fort Defiance South

POINT	MILES	DESCRIPTION
A	0.0	Exit Fort Defiance School Complex (elementary or middle school) and turn left onto Rt 616 Ft Defiance Rd heading away from Rt 11
B	0.6	Bear left on Rt 744 Leaport Rd
C	1.5	Continue right on Rt 742 Mt Pisgah Rd
D	1.9	Left on Rt 626 Limestone Rd
E	5.5	Left on Rt 612 Quicks Mill Rd
F	7.0	Cross Rt 11 Lee Hwy. Rt 612 Quicks Mill Rd becomes Laurel Hill Rd. Several stores along this section
G	7.1	Cross railroad tracks
H	8.0	Cross I-81. Caution: interchange
I	13.6	Left on Rt 608 Battlefield Rd. Store here
J	14.8	Left on Rt 616 Dam Town Rd. Turn is hidden between two houses
K	19.4	Cross I-81 on overpass (no interchange)
L	19.5	Cross railroad tracks
M	19.8	Cross Rt 11 Lee Hwy. Dam Town Rd becomes Ft Defiance Rd
A	20.2	Finish at Ft Defiance School Complex

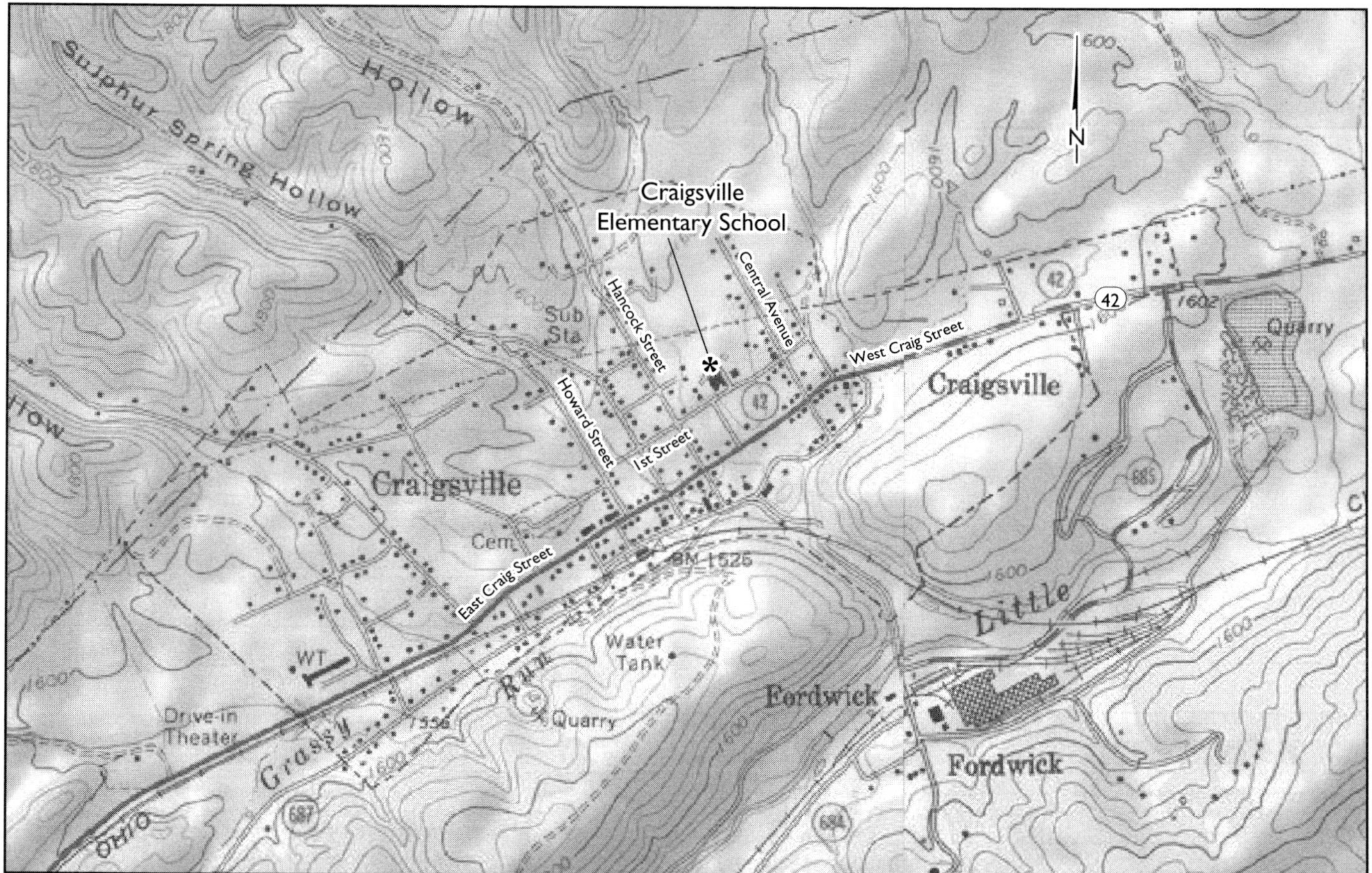

Craigsville
Elementary School
Hancock Street
Central Avenue
Howard Street
1st Street
West Craig Street
East Craig Street
Craigsville
Craigsville
Sub
Sta
Cem
BM 1526
Water
Tank
WT
Drive-in
Theater
Quarry
Quarry
Fordwick
Fordwick
Little
Run
Grassy
Sulphur Spring Hollow
Hollow
OHIO
42
N

Ride 21: Craigsville

Augusta Springs, Estaline, Fordwick

Ride through one of the more remote parts of western Augusta County and see interesting characteristics of small-town economies of yesterday and today. You will pass the empty and crumbling Portland Lehigh Cement Company, which was the economic mainstay of Craigsville before closing in 1968. Later in the ride, you pass a more modern source of income for rural areas: a large correctional facility. This ride is sandwiched between Great North and Little North Mountains and travels through what appears to be one of the poorest parts of the county.

DISTANCE 14.7 miles

ELEVATION CHANGE 745 feet

TRAFFIC LEVEL Very low, except on Route 42 Craig Street, which may carry frequent or high-speed traffic.

TERRAIN Flat at the start and finish, with some rolling hills in the middle as you circumnavigate Brown Ridge. About half the ride parallels small creeks.

STORES ALONG THE ROUTE None.

START LOCATION Craigsville Elementary School. From Staunton, head west on Route 250 Churchville Road to Churchville. At Churchville, take Route 42 Little Calf Pasture Highway south about 17 miles through Augusta Springs and into Craigsville. Turn right on Hancock Street. Go two blocks and turn right on 1st Street. Cross Johnson Street and park in the lot across from Craigsville Elementary School.

COMMENTS This ride is relatively far removed from most populated areas of Augusta County, so it will take a while to travel to the starting point. It is very different from the other rides in this book, so the time may be worthwhile if you are looking for an unusual riding experience.

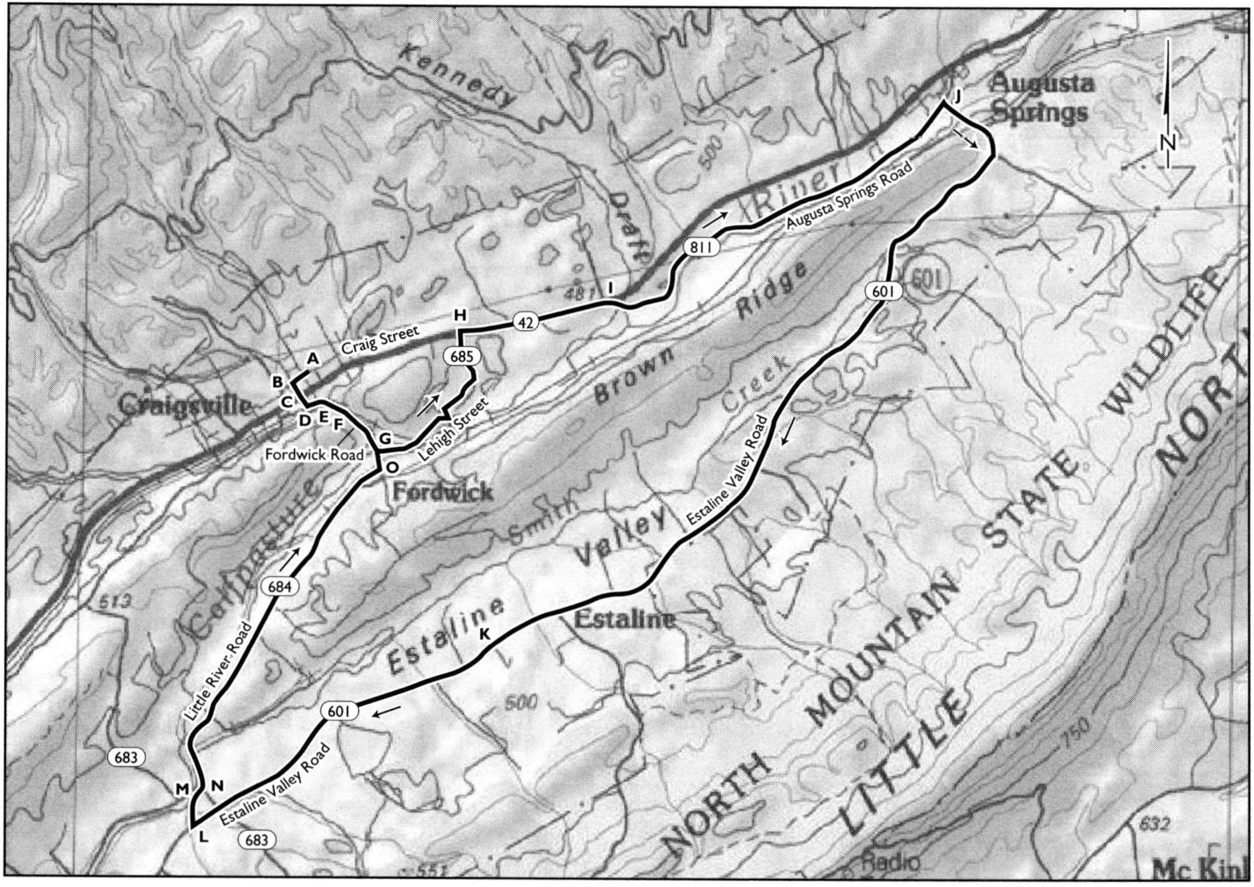
Augusta Springs
Craigsville
Fordwick
Estaline
Craig Street
Augusta Springs Road
Lehigh Street
Fordwick Road
Estaline Valley Road
Little River Road
42
685
811
601
684
683
A
B
C
D
E
F
G
H
I
J
K
L
M
N
O
N
Kennedy
River
Brown Ridge
Creek
Smith
Estaline Valley
Cowpasture
NORTH MOUNTAIN
LITTLE NORTH
STATE WILDLIFE
Radio

Ride 21: Craigsville

POINT	MILES	DESCRIPTION
A	0.0	Exit Craigsville Elementary School parking lot heading south on 1st St
B	0.05	Left on Hancock St
C	0.15	Cross Rt 42 W Craig St
D	0.20	Left on T687 Railroad Ave
E	0.25	Bear right on Fordwick Rd
F	0.35	Bear right on Fordwick Rd
G	0.60	Left on Lehigh St (becomes Rt 685). Pass Portland Lehigh Cement Co ruins
H	1.70	Right on Rt 42 W Craig St (becomes Little Calf Pasture Hwy)
I	2.50	Right on Rt 811 Augusta Springs Rd
J	4.90	Right on Rt 601 Estaline Valley Rd
K	9.60	Pass correctional facility
L	11.40	Right on Rt 684 Little River Rd
M	11.50	Continue straight on Rt 684/683 Little River Rd
N	11.60	Continue straight on Rt 684 Little River Rd
O	13.80	Bear left on Fordwick Rd
—	13.90	Pass Portland Lehigh Cement Co ruins
F	14.30	Bear left on Fordwick Rd
E	14.40	Bear left on T687 Railroad Ave
D	14.45	Right on Hancock St
C	14.50	Cross Rt 42 Craig St
B	14.60	Right on 1st St
A	14.65	Finish at Craigsville Elementary School

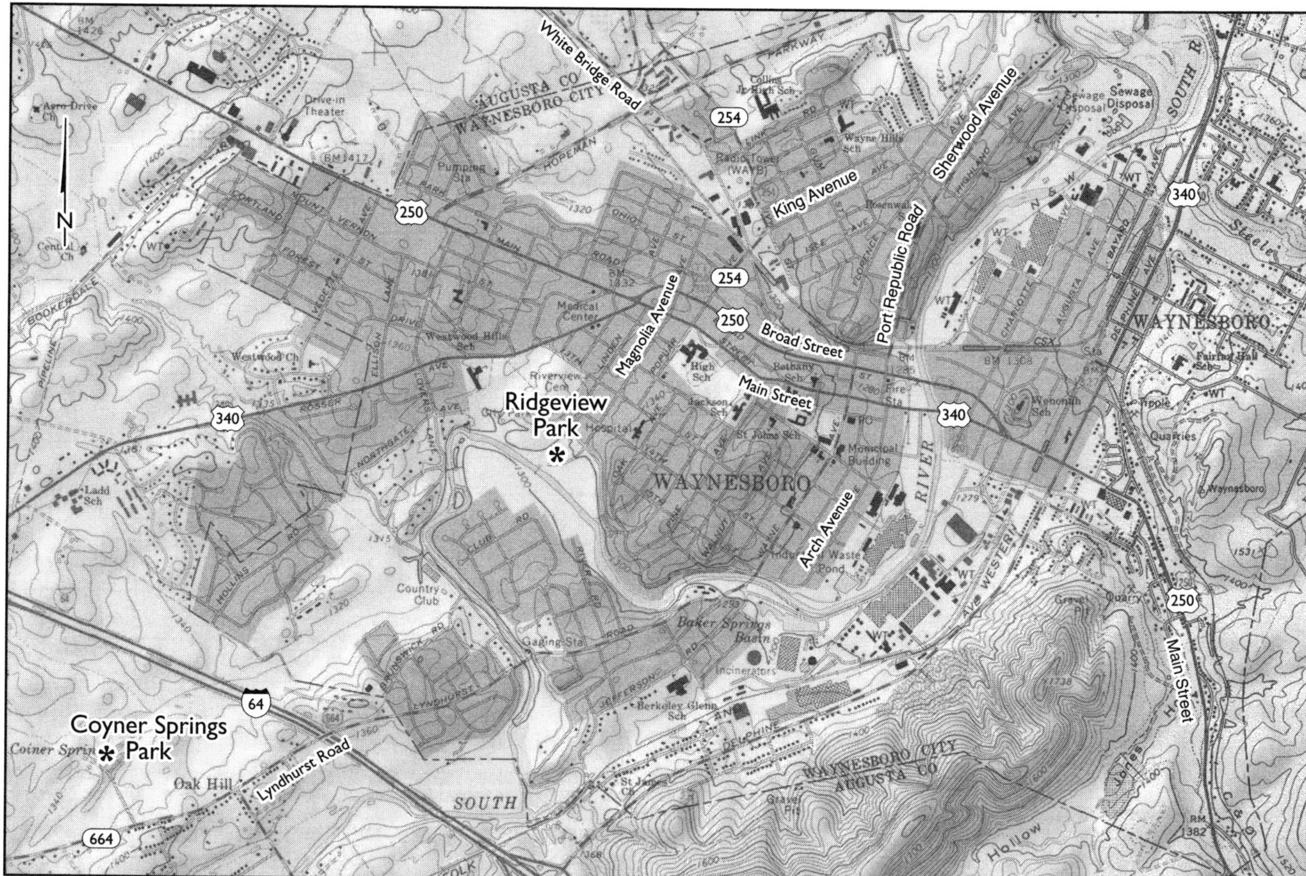
White Bridge Road
Sherwood Avenue
King Avenue
Port Republic Road
Broad Street
Main Street
Magnolia Avenue
Ridgeview Park
Arch Avenue
Main Street
Coyner Springs Park
Lyndhurst Road
WAYNESBORO
N

Ride 22: Waynesboro Northeast

Dooms

Travel from Waynesboro through the historic town of Dooms and along the lower western edge of Shenandoah National Park. Keep an eye out for Jarmans Gap Road turning off; this used to be one of the main roads through the Blue Ridge Mountains before the national park existed. This ride features more wooded, winding roads than the other rides from Waynesboro.

DISTANCE 15.0 miles

ELEVATION CHANGE 715 feet

TRAFFIC LEVEL Medium to high in and just outside of Waynesboro; low levels once out of town. Use caution on busy city streets and when crossing Hopeman Parkway and Route 340.

TERRAIN Rolling Shenandoah Valley terrain with some extra climbing as you work your way up to and through the foothills of the Blue Ridge Mountains.

STORES ALONG THE ROUTE None.

START LOCATION Ridgeview Park. From Route 340 West Main Street or Route 250 West Broad Street in downtown Waynesboro, turn south onto South Magnolia Avenue. Magnolia Avenue ends at Ridgeview Park, which has playing fields, a swimming pool, a picnic area, and other facilities.

COMMENTS This Waynesboro ride is unusual compared to the others in that it is more wooded and less open, and you get the feeling of riding through an older, less-developed rural hollow.

POINT	MILES	DESCRIPTION
A	0.0	Exit Ridgeview Park heading north on S Magnolia St
B	0.3	Right on 12th St
C	0.4	Left on Poplar Ave
D	0.6	Cross Rt 340 Main St
E	0.7	Cross Rt 250 Broad St
F	0.8	Cross railroad tracks
G	0.9	Straight on King Ave. Rt 254 Ivy St turns left here
H	1.4	Bear left on King Ave at intersection with Hemlock St and Dogwood St
I	1.6	Right on Bridge St
J	1.7	Left on Sherwood Ave
K	2.6	Cross Hopeman Pkwy

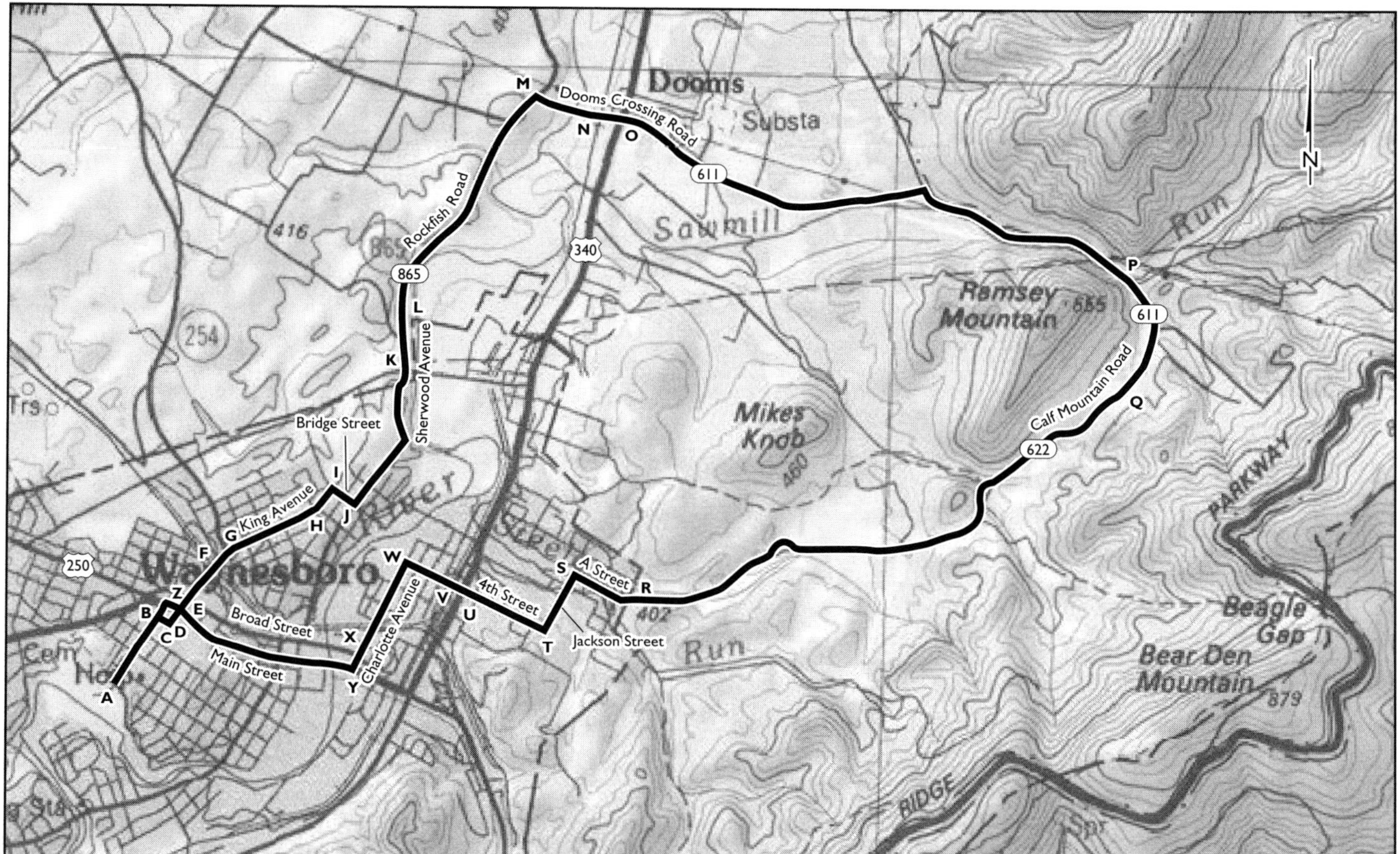
Dooms
Dooms Crossing Road
Substa
611
Rockfish Road
865
416
254
340
Sawmill
Run
Ramsey Mountain
855
Calf Mountain Road
622
Mikes Knob
460
Sherwood Avenue
Bridge Street
King Avenue
River
Waynesboro
250
Broad Street
Main Street
Charlotte Avenue
4th Street
A Street
Jackson Street
402
Run
Beagle Gap
Bear Den Mountain
879
PARKWAY
RIDGE
Trs
A
B
C
D
E
F
G
H
I
J
K
L
M
N
O
P
Q
R
S
T
U
V
W
X
Y
Z
N

Ride 22: Waynesboro Northeast

POINT	MILES	DESCRIPTION
L	2.7	Sherwood Ave becomes Rt 865 Rockfish Rd. Duike Rd turns off to the left. Continue straight through many small intersections
M	4.2	Right on Rt 611 Dooms Crossing Road
N	4.6	Cross railroad tracks
O	4.7	Cross Rt 340 at East Side Hwy
P	6.4	Straight on Rt 611 Calf Mountain Rd. Rt 619 Purple Cow Rd comes in from the left
Q	7.9	Bear right as Rt 611 becomes Rt 622 Calf Mountain Rd
R	11.4	Right on A St (may be unmarked)
S	11.7	Left on Jackson St
T	12.0	Right on 4th St
U	12.5	Cross Rt 340 Delphine Ave
V	12.6	Cross bridge
W	12.8	Left on Charlotte Ave
X	13.3	Cross Rt 250 Broad St
Y	13.4	Right on Rt 340 Main St
Z	14.4	Left on S Magnolia St
A	15.0	Finish at Ridgeview Park

Ride 23: Waynesboro North (long)

Madrid, Red Mills, Mount Meridian, Piedmont, New Hope, Kidville

Ride longitudinally up and down the Shenandoah Valley from Waynesboro, paralleling the base of the Blue Ridge Mountains with Skyline Drive running along the top of the ridge. Experience a mix of suburbia and rural farm country. This is a popular route from town, and you will likely meet other cyclists. There also are several shorter options.

DISTANCE 31.8 miles

ELEVATION CHANGE 850 feet

TRAFFIC LEVEL Medium to high in and just outside of Waynesboro; low levels once out of town. Use caution on Waynesboro streets, when crossing Hopeman Parkway, and when on or crossing Route 254.

TERRAIN Although this is one of the flatter rides in this book, the many rolling hills will wear you out if you tackle the full distance.

STORES ALONG THE ROUTE One, about two-thirds of the way through at the intersection of Route 612 New Hope and Crimora Road and Route 608 Battlefield Road.

START LOCATION Ridgeview Park. From Route 340 West Main Street or Route 250 West Broad Street in downtown Waynesboro, turn south onto South Magnolia Avenue. Magnolia Avenue ends at Ridgeview Park, which has playing fields, a swimming pool, a picnic area, and other facilities.

COMMENTS This is a classic ride from Waynesboro that can easily be cut shorter by taking any of the cross-valley roads as you travel north. These include New Hope and Crimora Road (for a 22-mile route), Humbert Road (25 miles), and Patterson Mill Road (28 miles). Turn left at any of these on the way out (points M, N, and O), and left again on Route 608 Battlefield Road (points Q, R, and S) to resume the route as described. All options are enjoyable in either direction.

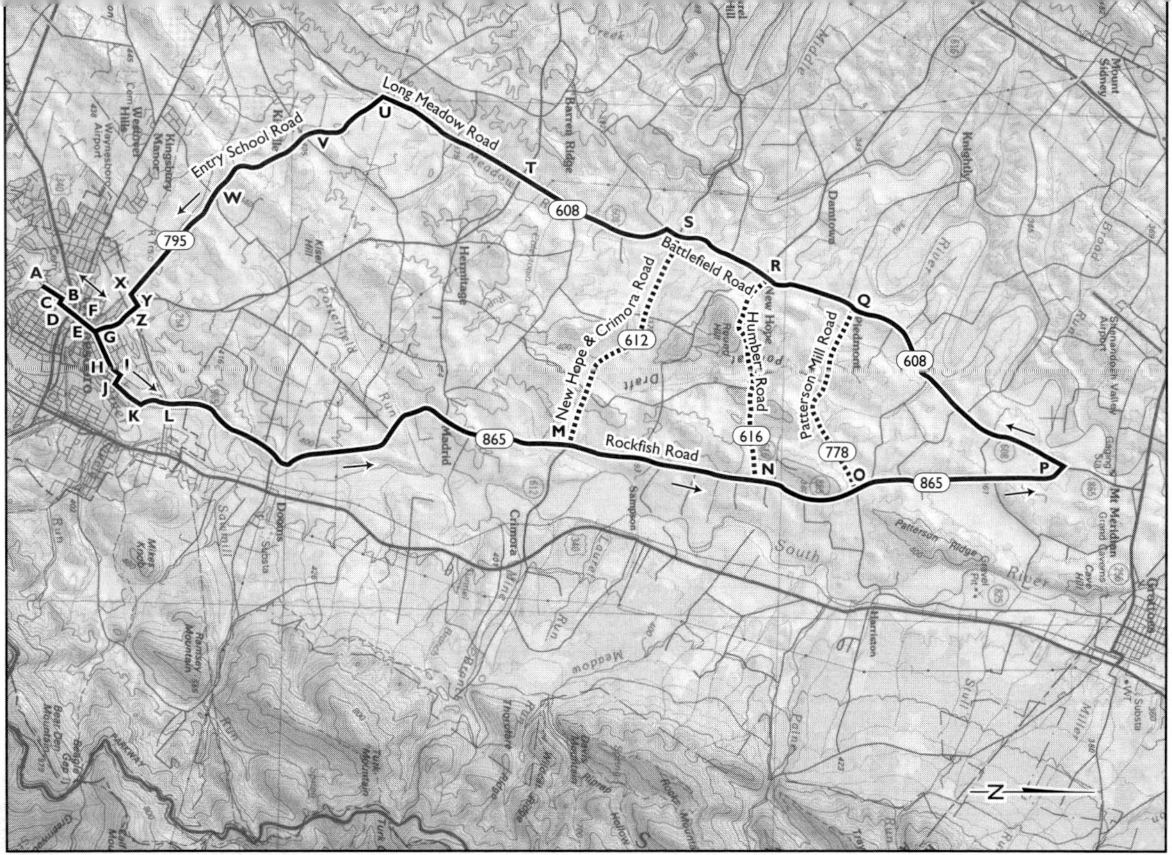

WAYNESBORO NORTH (LONG)

Ride 23: Waynesboro North (long)

POINT	MILES	DESCRIPTION
A	0.0	Exit Ridgeview Park heading north on South Magnolia St
B	0.3	Right on 12th St
C	0.4	Left on Poplar Ave
D	0.6	Cross Rt 340 Main St
E	0.7	Cross Rt 250 Broad St
F	0.8	Cross railroad tracks
G	0.9	Straight on King St. Rt 254 Ivy St turns left here
H	1.4	Bear left on King St at intersection with Hemlock St and Dogwood St
I	1.6	Right on Bridge St
J	1.7	Left on Sherwood Ave
K	2.6	Cross Hopeman Pkwy
L	2.7	Sherwood Ave becomes Rt 865 Rockfish Rd. Duike Rd turns off to the left. Continue straight through many small intersections
M	8.4	Continue straight on Rt 865 Rockfish Rd. For shortcut, turn left on Rt 612 New Hope and Crimora Rd
N	10.9	Continue straight on Rt 865 Rockfish Rd. For shortcut, turn left on Rt 616 Humbert Rd
O	12.3	Continue straight on Rt 865 Rockfish Rd. For shortcut, turn left on Rt 778 Patterson Mill Rd
P	15.1	Sharp left on Rt 608 Battlefield Rd
Q	18.7	Continue straight on Rt 608 Battlefield Rd. Rt 778 Patterson Mill Rd shortcut rejoins here
R	19.9	Continue straight on Rt 608 Battlefield Rd. Rt 616 Humbert Rd shortcut rejoins here
S	21.2	Rt 612 New Hope and Crimora Rd shortcut rejoins here. Store here

Ride 23: Waynesboro North (long)

POINT	MILES	DESCRIPTION
T	23.5	Cross Rt 254. Rt 608 Battlefield Rd becomes Rt 608 Long Meadow Rd
U	25.6	Left on Rt 795 Entry School Rd
V	26.8	Cross Rt 796 Kidville Rd
W	28.3	Cross Rt 640 Old White Bridge Rd. Rt 795 Entry School Rd eventually becomes White Bridge Rd
X	30.1	Sharp left on Guilford Ln (may not be marked)
Y	30.2	Right on Rt 254 Ivy St
Z	30.3	Cross Hopeman Pkwy
G	30.9	Right on Poplar Ave
F	31.0	Cross railroad tracks
E	31.1	Cross Rt 250 Broad St
D	31.2	Cross Rt 340 Main St
C	31.4	Right on 12th St
B	31.5	Left on S Magnolia St
A	31.8	Finish at Ridgeview Park

Ride 24: Waynesboro North (short)

Kidville, Hermitage, Madrid

Take a mellow spin on this relatively flat ride through open countryside. Although never far from town, you will enjoy quiet farmlands and suburbs and good views of sections of the valley. This is a great alternative to the longer Waynesboro North ride if you are short on time, fitness, or daylight hours.

DISTANCE 16.6 miles

ELEVATION CHANGE 505 feet

TRAFFIC LEVEL Medium to high in and just outside of Waynesboro; low levels once out of town. Use caution on Waynesboro streets, when crossing Hopeman Parkway, and when on or crossing Route 254.

TERRAIN Relatively flat with some good rolling hills, but a small amount of climbing overall for a ride of this distance.

STORES ALONG THE ROUTE None.

START LOCATION Ridgeview Park. From Route 340 West Main Street or Route 250 West Broad Street in downtown Waynesboro, turn south onto South Magnolia Avenue. Magnolia Avenue ends at Ridgeview Park, which has playing fields, a swimming pool, a picnic area, and other facilities.

COMMENTS This shorter version of the Waynesboro North (long) ride runs in the opposite direction for variety's sake, but can be ridden enjoyably in either direction.

WAYNESBORO NORTH (SHORT)

Ride 24: Waynesboro North (short)

POINT	MILES	DESCRIPTION
A	0.0	Exit Ridgeview Park heading north on S Magnolia St
B	0.3	Right on 12th St
C	0.4	Left on Poplar Ave
D	0.6	Cross Rt 340 Main St
E	0.7	Cross Rt 250 Broad St
F	0.8	Cross railroad tracks
G	0.9	Left on Rt 254 Ivy St
H	1.5	Cross Hopeman Pkwy
I	1.6	Left on Guilford Ln (may not be marked)
J	1.7	Right on Rt 795 White Bridge Rd (becomes Entry School Rd)
K	3.5	Cross Rt 640 Old White Bridge Rd
L	5.0	Right on Rt 796 Kidville Rd
M	6.9	Left on Rt 254 (becomes Rt 796 Oak Grove Church Rd)
N	7.6	Right on Rt 619 Hildebrand Church Rd
O	9.9	Right on Rt 865 Rockfish Rd
P	14.1	Cross Hopeman Pkwy. Rt 865 Rockfish Rd becomes Sherwood Ave, then Port Republic Rd
Q	14.9	Right on Bridge St
R	15.0	Left on King St
G	15.7	King St becomes Poplar Ave
F	15.9	Cross railroad tracks
E	16.0	Right on Rt 250 Broad St
D	16.1	Cross Rt 340 Main St
C	16.2	Right on 12th St
B	16.3	Left on S Magnolia St
A	16.6	Finish at Ridgeview Park

Ride 25: Waynesboro South (short)

Lyndhurst, Lipscomb

This short ride is ideal for beginners because there are no major hills and not much traffic. The roads are fairly straight so cars can pass easily, but riders still get to enjoy views of the mountains on a loop close to town. You will see signs of the industrialization of this area, but you will stay away from the warehouses and the truck traffic associated with them.

DISTANCE 10.3 miles

ELEVATION CHANGE 145 feet

TRAFFIC LEVEL Low, except on the section of Route 664 Lyndhurst Road just outside the park, where traffic may be moderate to heavy.

TERRAIN Mostly flat.

STORES ALONG THE ROUTE None.

START LOCATION Coyner Springs Park. From Route 340 in downtown Waynesboro, turn south on Wayne Avenue. Travel 0.3 miles and cross Rife Road/Arch Avenue. Continue straight on Lyndhurst Road (becomes Route 664) an additional 2.2 miles. Turn right into Coyner Springs Park.

OR

From I-64, exit at Route 340 South Stuarts Draft Highway. About 0.8 miles south of the interchange, turn left onto Route 631 Ladd Road. Travel 1.5 miles straight on this road, which becomes Route 664 Lyndhurst Road about halfway there, and turn left into Coyner Springs Park after about 1.5 miles.

COMMENTS Riders can add distance by riding 2.5 miles to the starting location from downtown Waynesboro instead of driving. It is mostly uphill, and there may be significant traffic. See also the Waynesboro South (long) ride for an extended and slightly more advanced version of this ride.

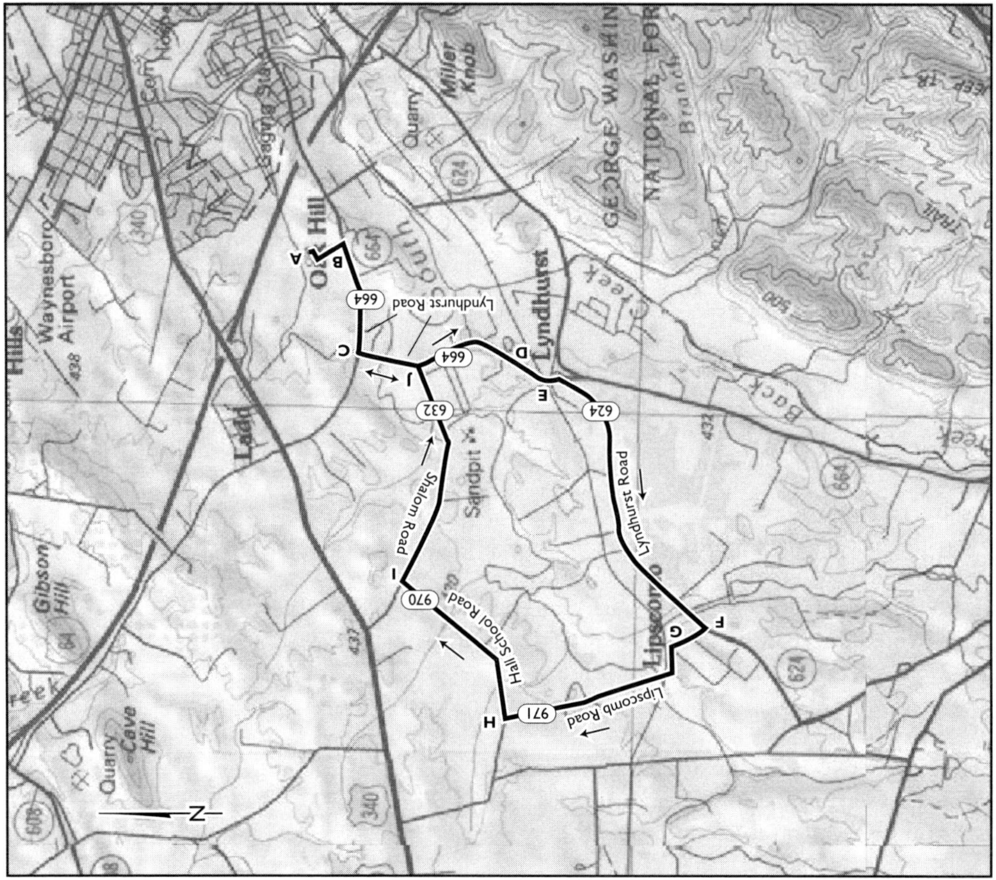

A
B
C
D
E
F
G
H
I
J
664
632
624
970
971
Lyndhurst Road
Shalom Road
Hall School Road
Lipscomb Road
Lyndhurst
Waynesboro Airport
Gibson Hill
Cave Hill
Quarry
Sandpit
Miller Knob
GEORGE WASHINGTON NATIONAL FOREST
Back Creek
Ladd
340
N

Ride 25: Waynesboro South (short)

POINT	MILES	DESCRIPTION
A	0.0	Exit Coyner Springs Park
B	0.3	Right on Rt 664 Lyndhurst Rd
C	1.0	Left on Rt 664 Lyndhurst Rd
D	2.4	Cross railroad tracks
E	2.5	Right on Rt 624 Lyndhurst Rd
F	4.5	Right on Rt 971 Lipscomb Rd
G	5.0	Cross railroad tracks
H	6.1	Right on Rt 970 Hall School Rd
I	7.4	Right on Rt 632 Shalom Rd
J	8.9	Left on Rt 664 Lyndhurst Rd
C	9.3	Right on Rt 664 Lyndhurst Rd
B	10.0	Left into Coyner Springs Park
A	10.3	Finish at Coyner Springs Park

Ride 26: Waynesboro South (long)

Lyndhurst, Sherando, Lipscomb

Although never climbing any of the surrounding mountains, riders will enjoy them as part of the scenery. They also have the option to take a detour to the popular Sherando Recreational Area within George Washington National Forest. When riding south through the town of Sherando, riders can see the Blue Ridge Parkway meandering along the ridge to the east.

DISTANCE 15.7 miles

ELEVATION CHANGE 325 feet

TRAFFIC LEVEL Low on most roads, but may be moderate to heavy on the section of Route 664 Lyndhurst Road just outside Coyner Springs Park, on Route 664 Mount Torrey Road, and on Route 610 Howardsville Turnpike.

TERRAIN This ride is one of the flattest you can do in the Shenandoah Valley.

STORES ALONG THE ROUTE One, at the intersection of Route 664 Mount Torrey Road and Route 610 Howardsville Turnpike in the town of Sherando.

START LOCATION Coyner Springs Park. From Route 340 in downtown Waynesboro, turn south on Wayne Avenue. Travel 0.3 miles and cross Rife Road/Arch Avenue. Continue straight on Lyndhurst Road (becomes Route 664) 2.2 miles. Turn right into Coyner Springs Park.

OR

From I-64, exit at Route 340 South Stuarts Draft Highway. About 0.8 miles south of the interchange, turn left onto Route 631 Ladd Road. Travel 1.5 miles straight on this road, which becomes Route 664 Lyndhurst Road about halfway there, and turn left into Coyner Springs Park after about 1.5 miles.

COMMENTS This ride is a longer version of the Waynesboro South (short) ride also leaving from Coyner Springs. Riders can add distance by riding 2.5 miles to the starting location from downtown Waynesboro instead of driving. It is mostly uphill, and there may be significant traffic. Riders may also add distance and do some sight-seeing by continuing four miles south on Route 664 Mount Torrey Road past the town of Sherando toward the Sherando Recreational Area. It's another mile or two into the area, where there are camping, picnicking, and swimming options.

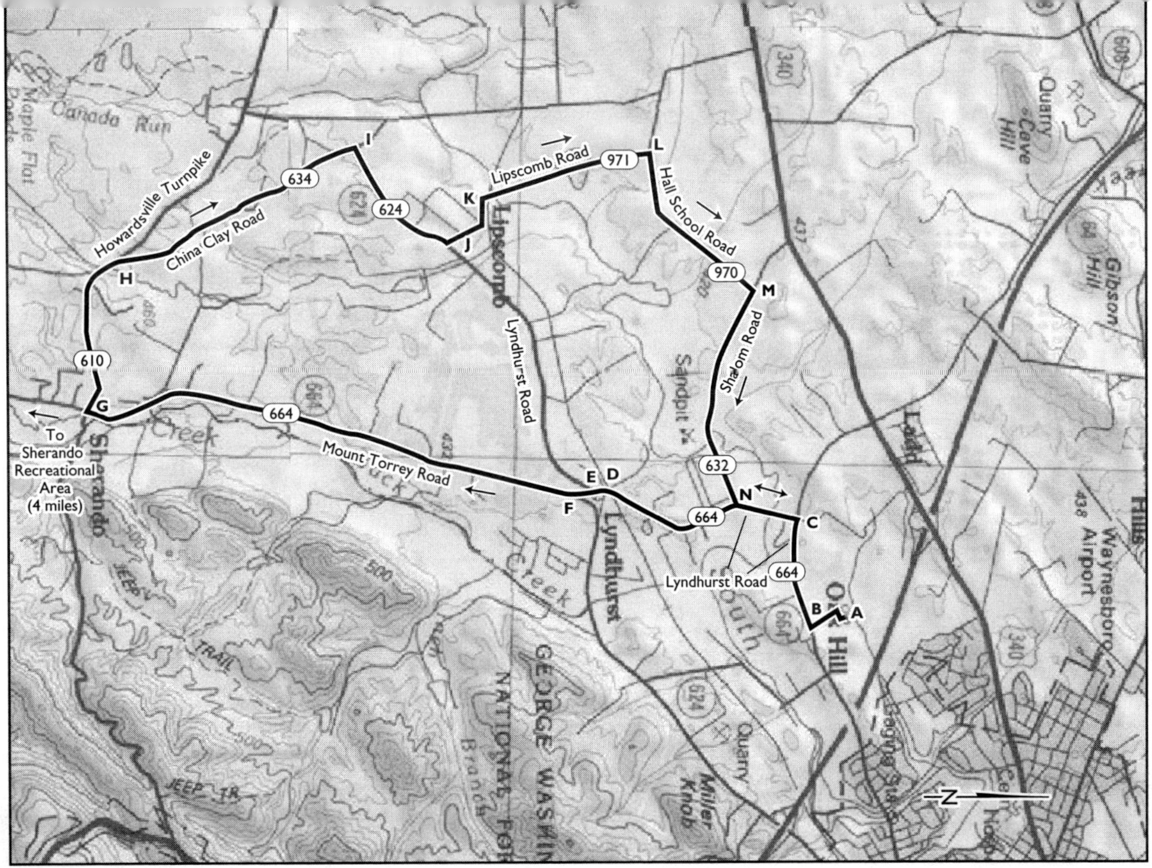

WAYNESBORO SOUTH (LONG)

Ride 26: Waynesboro South (long)

POINT	MILES	DESCRIPTION
A	0.0	Exit Coyner Springs Park
B	0.3	Right on Rt 664 Lyndhurst Rd
C	1.0	Left on Rt 664 Lyndhurst Rd
D	2.4	Cross railroad tracks
E	2.5	Continue straight and pass turnoff to the right for Rt 624 Lyndhurst Rd. Waynesboro South (short) ride turns here
F	2.6	Right on Rt 664 Mt Torrey Rd
G	6.1	Right on Rt 610 Howardsville Turnpike
H	7.2	Right at Y on Rt 634 China Clay Rd
I	9.0	Right on Rt 624 Lyndhurst Rd
J	9.9	Left on Rt 971 Lipscomb Rd. Waynesboro South (short) ride rejoins here
K	10.4	Cross railroad tracks
L	11.5	Right on Rt 970 Hall School Rd
M	12.8	Right on Rt 632 Shalom Rd
N	14.3	Left on Rt 664 Lyndhurst Rd
C	14.7	Right on Rt 664 Lyndhurst Rd
B	15.4	Left into Coyner Springs Park
A	15.7	Finish at Coyner Springs Park

Ride 27: Stuarts Draft

Cold Spring, Spottswood, Greenville

This route travels generally south along the edge of the area of George Washington National Forest known as Big Levels. Riders looking for a much shorter option (about 19.5 miles) can cut off at Cold Springs, while distance-oriented riders can head farther south and tour through Spottswood on some lovely, little-traveled back roads. All riders get to return on Indian Ridge, a great longitudinal ridge that offers views in all directions. Look to the east to see the scree slopes on the steep mountainsides of Big Levels.

DISTANCE 35.8 miles

ELEVATION CHANGE 1,415 feet

TRAFFIC LEVEL Moderate to heavy in and near Stuarts Draft on Route 608 Draft Avenue and Route 608 Cold Spring Road. Watch out for truck traffic near the industrial plants on Route 608 Draft Avenue. Low levels everywhere else.

TERRAIN Typical Shenandoah Valley rolling terrain with many hills throughout.

STORES ALONG THE ROUTE None.

START LOCATION Stuarts Draft Park. From I-64, exit at Fisherville on Route 340 South. Go about 5.5 miles. Turn left on Route 608 Draft Avenue toward Stuarts Draft. After about 0.7 miles, turn left on Route 639 Wayne Avenue. Go 0.2 miles and turn right into Stuarts Draft Park.

COMMENTS For the shorter, 19.5-mile loop, turn right at Route 662 Greenville School Road (point G). Continue for 1.6 miles to Greenville. Turn right on Main Street and rejoin the route by taking a right onto Route 657 Indian Ridge Road (point S). Note that in Greenville, Route 11 and Main Street run parallel to each other, and Route 657 Indian Ridge Road turns off Main Street, not Route 11.

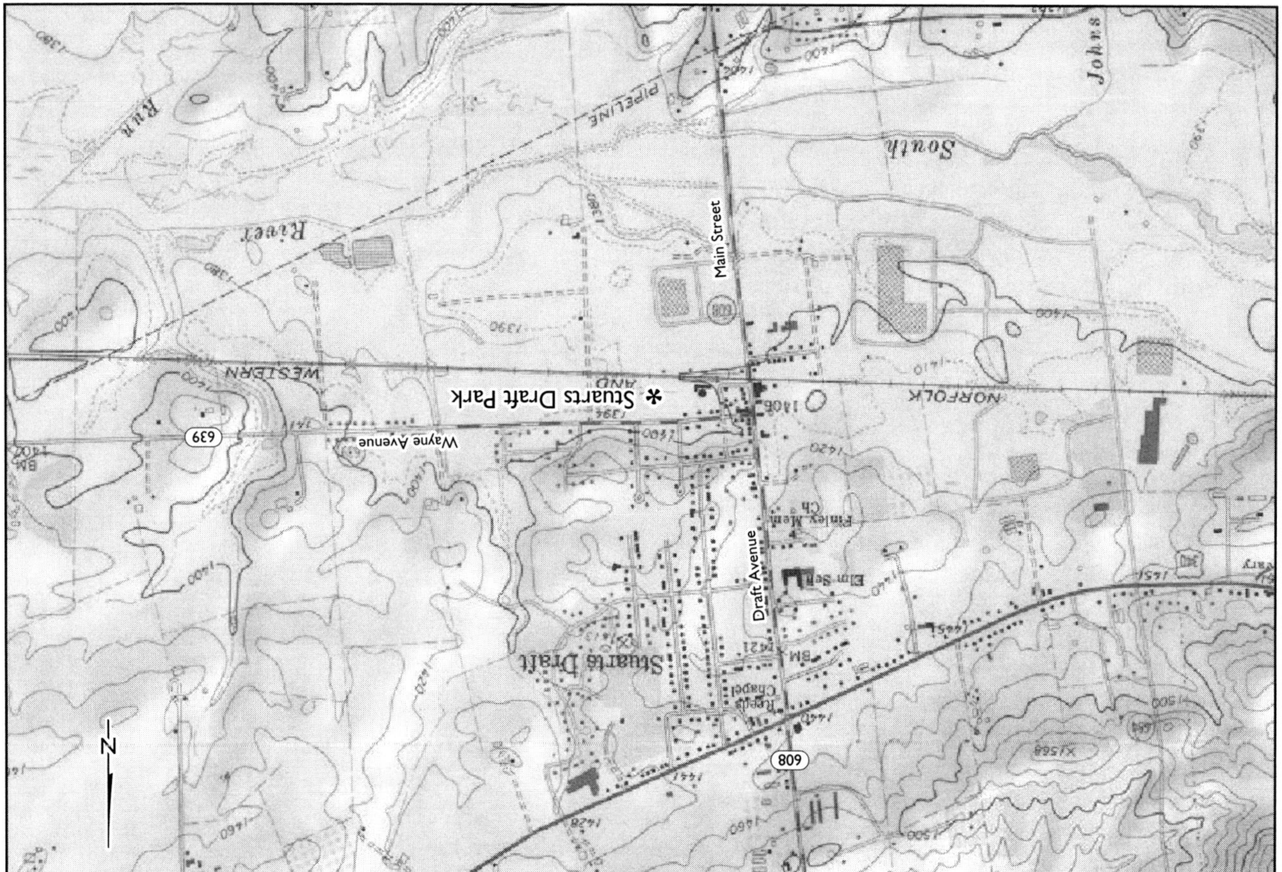
Stuarts Draft Park
Main Street
Draft Avenue
Wayne Avenue
639
809
N
Stuarts Draft
NORFOLK
WESTERN
PIPELINE
South
River

Ride 27: Stuarts Draft

POINT	MILES	DESCRIPTION
A	0.0	Exit Stuarts Draft Park to left on Rt 639 Wayne Ave
B	0.2	Left on Rt 608 Draft Ave
C	0.3	Cross railroad tracks
D	1.0	Right on Rt 608 Cold Spring Rd
E	1.1	Bear right on Rt 608 Cold Spring Rd
F	3.2	Bear left on Rt 608 Cold Spring Rd
G	8.1	Straight on Rt 608 Cold Spring Rd. Turn right on Rt 662 Greenville School Rd for shortcut
H	9.6	Bear right on Rt 608 Cold Spring Rd
I	13.6	Right on Rt 667 Dabneys Rd just after railroad underpass
J	15.8	Left on Rt 11 Lee Jackson Hwy
K	16.4	Right on Rt 620 Spottswood Dr
L	17.9	Cross I-81/I-64 (no interchange)
M	19.1	Right on Rt 919 Old Providence Rd
N	22.4	Left on Rt 675 Broadhead School Rd
O	22.9	Right on Rt 604 McClures Mill Rd
P	24.2	Right on Rt 662 Stover School Rd
Q	25.1	Cross I-81/I-64 (no interchange)
R	25.8	Cross Rt 11 Lee Jackson Hwy
S	25.9	Left on Rt 1205 Main St. Shortcut rejoins here
T	26.0	Right on Rt 657 Indian Ridge Rd
U	31.8	Right on Rt 656 Offliter Rd
V	32.0	Cross railroad tracks
F	32.5	Left on Rt 608 Cold Spring Rd
D	34.8	Left on Rt 608 Draft Ave
C	35.5	Cross railroad tracks
B	35.6	Right on Rt 639 Wayne Ave
A	35.8	Finish at Stuarts Draft Park

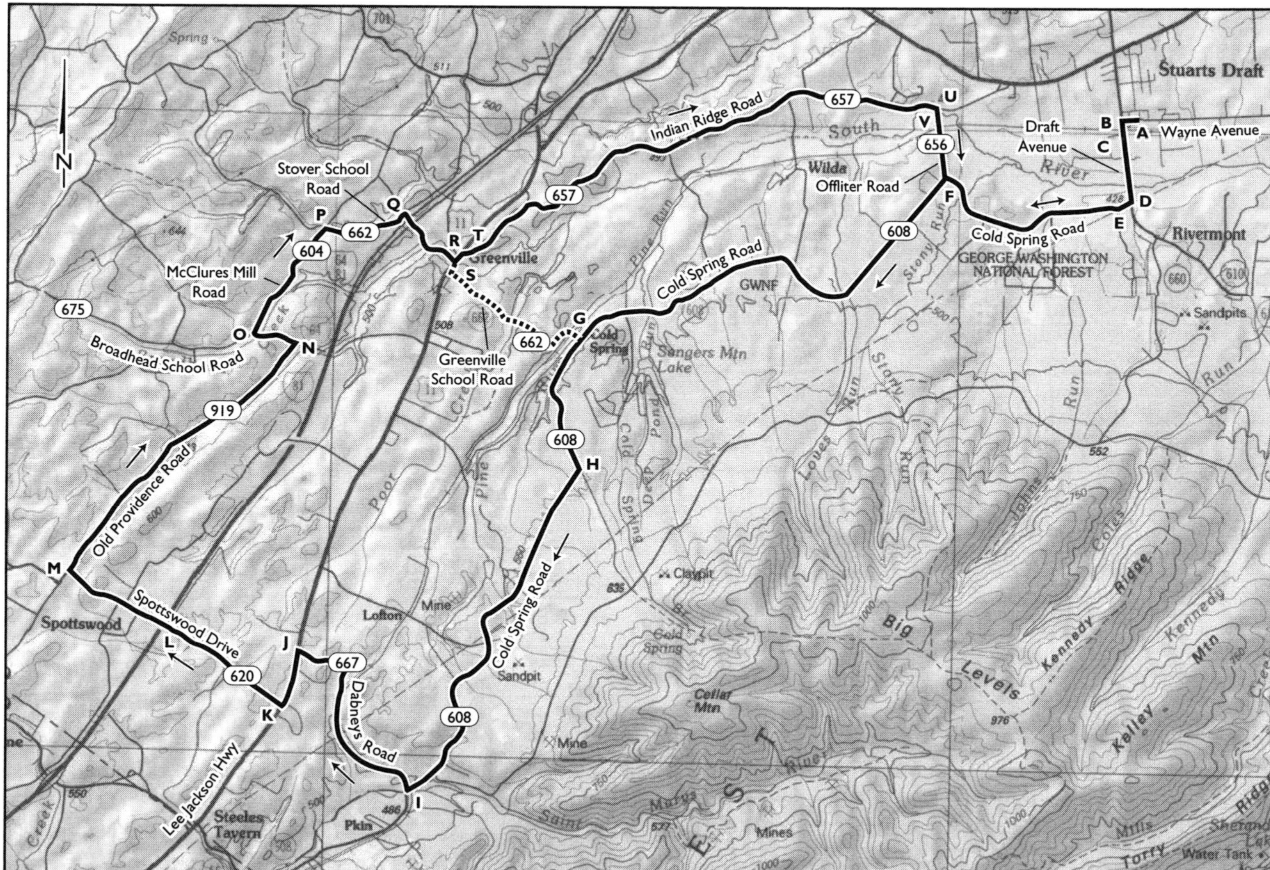

Stuarts Draft
Wayne Avenue
Draft Avenue
Offliter Road
Cold Spring Road
Rivermont
GEORGE WASHINGTON NATIONAL FOREST
GWNF
Indian Ridge Road
Stover School Road
McClures Mill Road
Broadhead School Road
Greenville
Greenville School Road
Old Providence Road
Spottswood
Spottswood Drive
Lee Jackson Hwy
Steeles Tavern
Dabneys Road
Sangers Mtn
Cellar Mtn
Big Levels
Kennedy Ridge
Kelley Mtn
N

Albemarle County

rides leaving from

Charlottesville

Earlysville

Stony Point

Red Hill, Walnut Creek, and Carters Bridge

Esmont

Greenwood

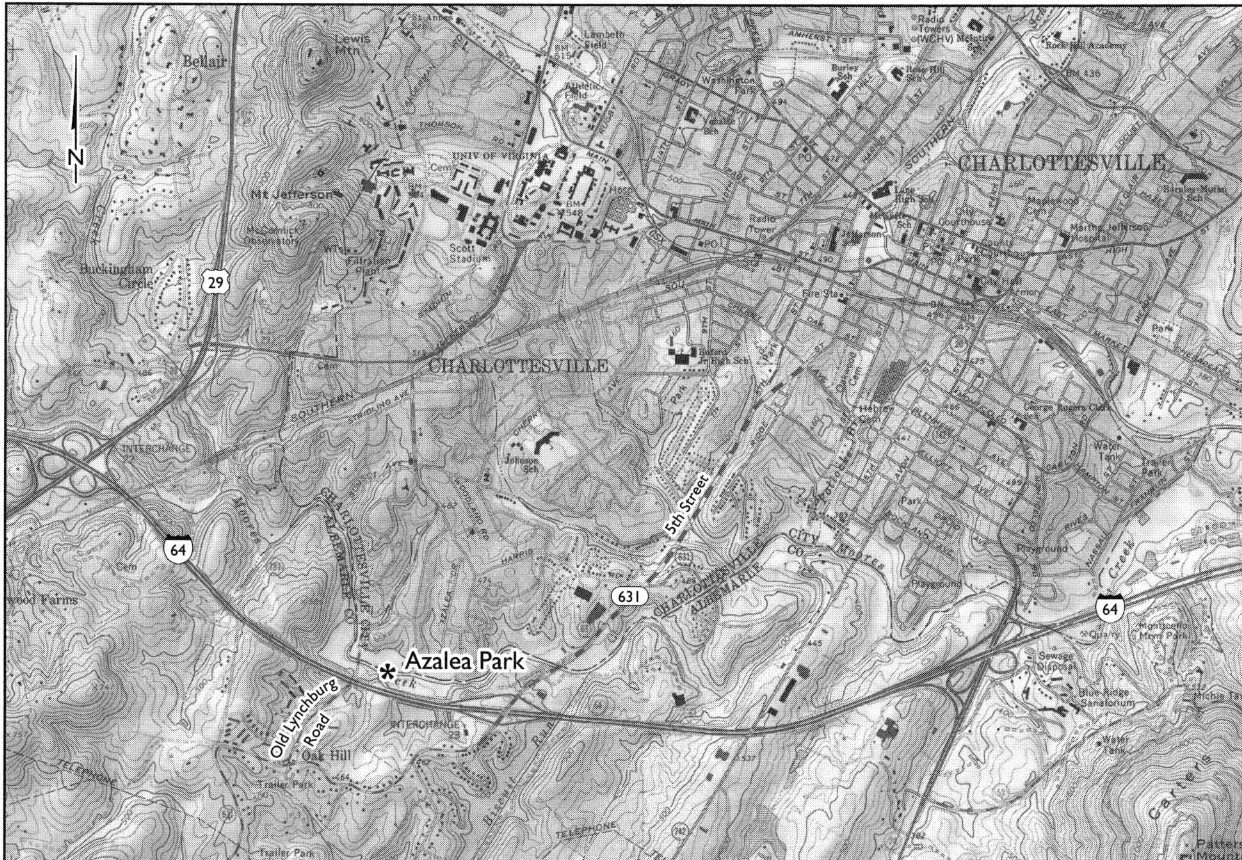
Azalea Park
5th Street
Old Lynchburg Road
631
64
29
CHARLOTTESVILLE
UNIV OF VIRGINIA
Mt Jefferson
Lewis Mtn
Bellair
N

Ride 28: Charlottesville South

Red Hill, Dudley Mountain

This short but popular lollipop-shaped loop can be squeezed in before or after work or between classes. It features some short, steep hills as well as rolling hills.

DISTANCE 14.8 miles

ELEVATION CHANGE 865 feet

TRAFFIC LEVEL Moderate to heavy, especially on Old Lynchburg Road and at rush hour. The road is narrow and twisty and lined with driveways and subdivision entrances. Traffic may be moving fast on some sections. This is a main route south from town for both cars and bikes.

TERRAIN Rolling, with some steep hills on the way in and out of town.

STORES ALONG THE ROUTE None.

START LOCATION Azalea Park. Exit I-64 at Charlottesville's 5th Street and head south for about 0.7 miles. Turn right onto Old Lynchburg Road. Azalea Park is on the right after about 0.5 miles, just after you cross under I-64.

COMMENTS Constant development in this area means more and more traffic. If you're looking for a longer ride from Charlottesville, start on this route, then link to the Red Hill Southeast ride in reverse (point E on this route; point I on that route) to do the local favorite North Garden loop. These two rides overlap on Route 708 Red Hill Road. University-based riders may start at Alderman Road to add about five miles total. Head south as the road becomes Maury Avenue and Jefferson Park Avenue Extended, then turn right on Old Lynchburg Road and head toward Azalea Park.

POINT	MILES	DESCRIPTION
A	0.0	Exit Azalea Park by going left on Old Lynchburg Rd
B	0.1	Cross I-64 (no interchange). Old Lynchburg Rd becomes Rt 780 Old Lynchburg Rd
C	0.5	Right on Rt 631 Old Lynchburg Rd
D	2.9	Straight on Rt 631 Old Lynchburg Rd
E	7.0	Right on Rt 708 Red Hill Rd. Caution: Steep, twisty descent
F	8.0	Sharp right on Rt 706 Dudley Mtn Rd
D	11.9	Left on Rt 631 Old Lynchburg Rd
C	14.3	Left on Rt 780 Old Lynchburg Rd
B	14.7	Cross I-64 (no interchange)
A	14.8	Right to finish at Azalea Park

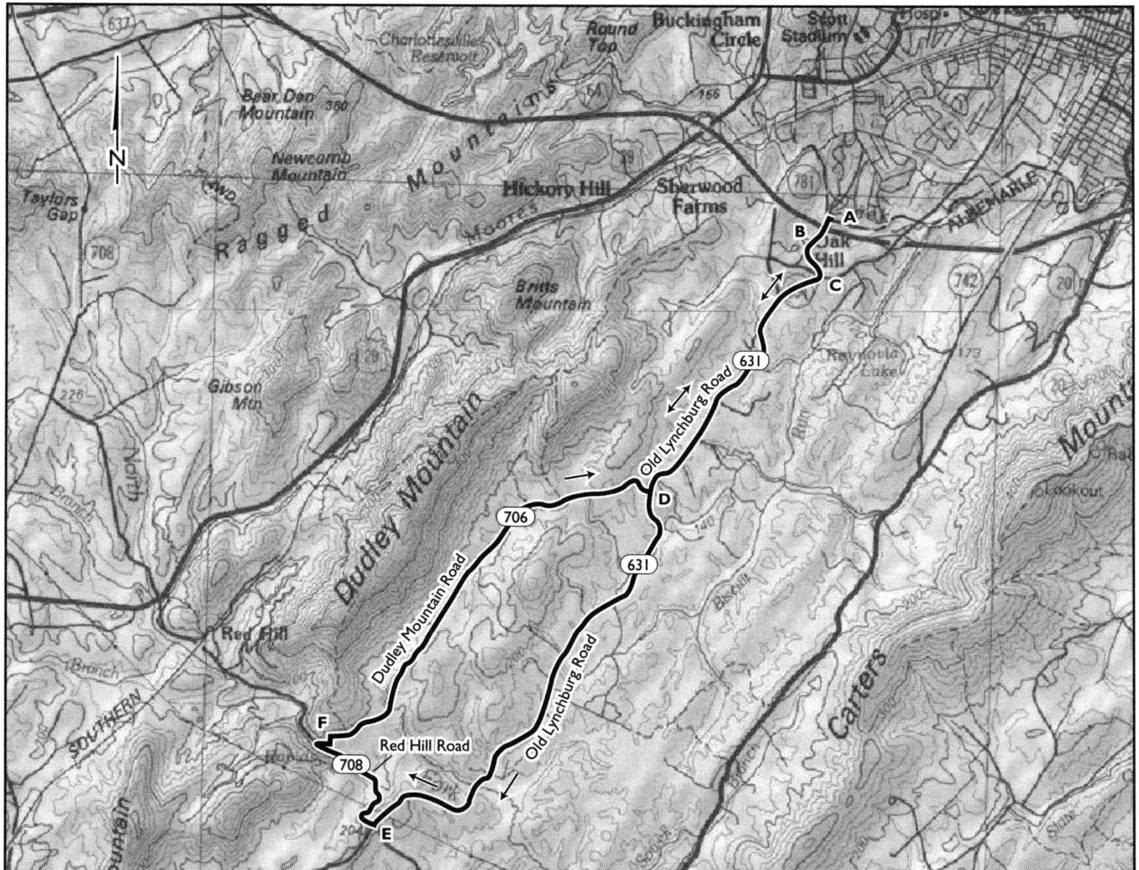

A
B
C
D
E
F
631
706
708
Old Lynchburg Road
Dudley Mountain Road
Red Hill Road
Dudley Mountain
Ragged Mountains
Carters
Hickory Hill
Sherwood Farms
Buckingham Circle
Scott Stadium
Round Top
Charlottesville Reservoir
Bear Den Mountain
Newcomb Mountain
Taylors Gap
Britts Mountain
Gibson Mtn
Red Hill
Oak Hill
Moores
SOUTHERN
ALBEMARLE
N

Ride 29: Charlottesville Northwest

Owensville, Farmington

This ride features a brief stretch of the famous cross-country Bikecentennial route from 1976 and takes you past a local landmark called Foxfield, where horse races are held every spring and fall. In the spring, you will see beautiful pink, white, and purple flowering trees everywhere. Some roads on this ride are busy, but this is still a good, short route from town for those riders comfortable in traffic.

DISTANCE 20.1 miles

ELEVATION CHANGE 800 feet

TRAFFIC LEVEL Moderate to heavy heading in and out of Charlottesville, especially at rush hour and when on or crossing Route 250 Ivy Road and Route 601/676 Garth Road. Route 250 is usually busy, but this short section is fairly wide and straight and has a shoulder in places. City streets have plenty of vehicle and pedestrian traffic near the University of Virginia.

TERRAIN Hilly, with more climbing on the way out than the way back.

STORES ALONG THE ROUTE None outside of town.

START LOCATION Azalea Park. Exit I-64 at Charlottesville's 5th Street and head south for about 0.7 miles. Turn right onto Old Lynchburg Road. Azalea Park is on the right after about 0.5 miles, just after you cross under I-64.

COMMENTS This ride is the main route out of town to the northwest and can be linked with rides from Earlysville by taking a right on Route 601 Free Union Road (point J). There is significant traffic at all times of the day, but especially during morning and evening rush hours. However, because of its proximity to the university, this ride is a favorite among those looking for a quick trip. University-based riders may start at Alderman Road and join the route between points D and E. When starting from the university, the ride is significantly shorter at about 15 miles total.

Old Lynchburg Road
Jefferson Park Avenue
Alderman Road
Old Ivy Road
Ivy Road
Old Garth Road
Garth Road
601
676
677
Old Ballard Road
Owensville Road
Owensville
West Leigh
Flordon
Bellair
Buckingham Circle
Round Top
Sherwood Farms
Hickory Hill
Montvue
Canterbury Hills
Cotthurst
Stillhouse Mountain
Radio Towers
Jumping Branch
South Fork Rivanna River Reservoir
Charlottesville Reservoir
Oak Hill
A
B
C
D
E
F
G
H
I
J
K
L
M
N
O
N

Ride 29: Charlottesville Northwest

POINT	MILES	DESCRIPTION
A	0.0	Exit Azalea Park by going right on Old Lynchburg Rd
B	0.7	Left on Jefferson Park Ave Extended
C	1.2	Continue straight. Jefferson Park Ave becomes Maury Ave
D	1.5	Continue straight. Maury Ave becomes Alderman Rd
E	2.6	Left on Business Rt 250 Ivy Rd
F	2.8	Bear right at yield on Old Ivy Rd
G	3.5	Cross Rt 250 Bypass at interchange
H	3.6	Continue straight on Rt 601 Old Garth Rd
I	5.7	Left on Rt 601 Garth Rd. Join 1976 Bikecentennial route here.
J	8.5	Straight on Rt 676 Garth Rd
K	9.6	Left on Rt 676 Owensville Rd. Leave 1976 Bikecentennial route here
L	11.1	Left on Rt 677 Old Ballard Rd
M	14.7	Cross railroad tracks. Road bears right and becomes Broomley Rd
N	14.8	Left on Rt 250 Ivy Rd
O	16.7	Cross Rt 29 Bypass (caution: interchange)
E	17.5	Right on Alderman Rd
D	18.6	Continue straight. Alderman Rd becomes Maury Ave
C	18.9	Continue straight. Maury Ave becomes Jefferson Park Ave Extended
B	19.4	Right on Old Lynchburg Rd
A	20.1	Left to finish at Azalea Park

Ride 30: Charlottesville West

Red Hill, Taylors Gap, Bloomfield

Enjoy the rolling hills to the west and south of Charlottesville and finish by riding through the University of Virginia campus. The ride takes you past old, modest houses as well as through newer, wealthier neighborhoods in Albemarle County. You will encounter traffic getting in and out of town, but will enjoy quiet secondary roads mid-ride. In the summer, riders will enjoy the fact that this route offers plenty of shade.

DISTANCE 24.3 miles

ELEVATION CHANGE 1,315 feet

TRAFFIC LEVEL Moderate to heavy heading in and out of Charlottesville, especially at rush hour and when on or crossing Old Lynchburg Road, Route 29 Monacan Trail, and Route 250 Ivy Road. Old Lynchburg Road is narrow and twisty and lined with driveways and subdivision entrances. Route 250 Ivy Road is usually busy, but this short section is fairly wide and straight and has a shoulder in places. Also use caution on city streets, which have plenty of vehicle and pedestrian traffic near the University of Virginia.

TERRAIN Hilly, with more climbing on the way out than the way back.

STORES ALONG THE ROUTE None outside of town.

START LOCATION Azalea Park. Exit I-64 at Charlottesville's 5th Street and head south for about 0.7 miles. Turn right onto Old Lynchburg Road. Azalea Park is on the right after about 0.5 miles, just after you cross under I-64.

COMMENTS Although the rider taking this route during evening rush hour will be traveling the opposite way of most traffic on Route 250, the ride can be enjoyable in either direction during quieter hours. University-based riders may start at Alderman Road between points M and N and head out past the Azalea Park starting point.

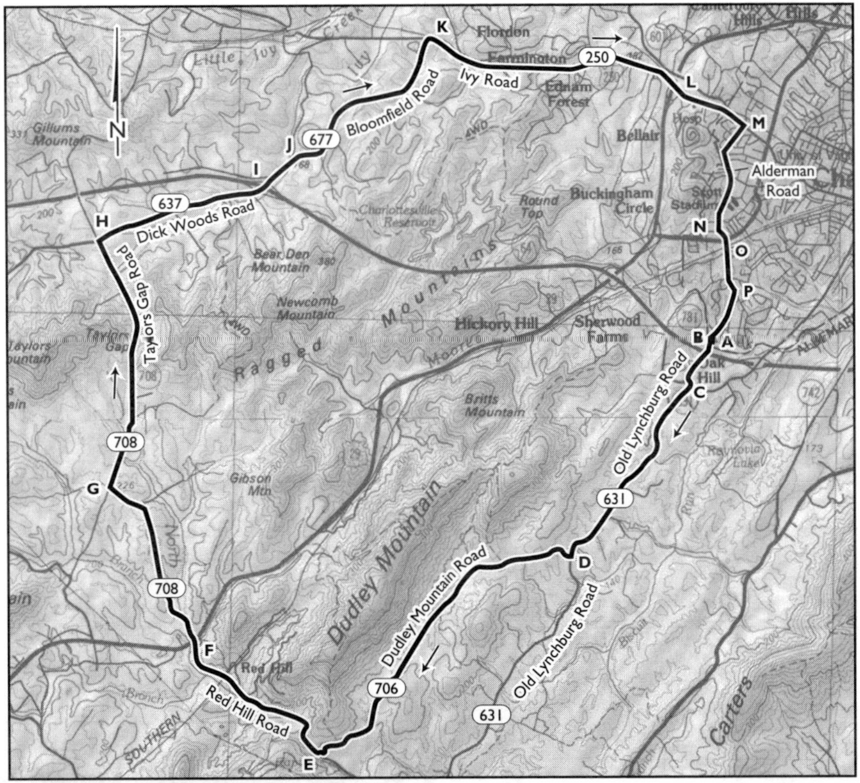

CHARLOTTESVILLE WEST

Ride 30: Charlottesville West

POINT	MILES	DESCRIPTION
A	0.0	Exit Azalea Park by going left on Old Lynchburg Rd
B	0.1	Cross I-64 (no interchange). Old Lynchburg Rd becomes Rt 780 Old Lynchburg Rd
C	0.5	Right on Rt 631 Old Lynchburg Rd
D	2.9	Right on Rt 706 Dudley Mtn Rd
E	6.8	Right on Rt 708 Red Hill Rd
F	8.9	Cross Rt 29 Monacan Trail
G	10.8	Right on Rt 708 Taylors Gap Rd
H	13.6	Right on Rt 637 Dick Woods Rd
I	15.4	Cross I-64 (caution: interchange)
J	15.9	Right on Rt 677 Bloomfield Rd
K	18.0	Right on Rt 250 Ivy Rd
L	20.9	Cross Rt 29 Bypass (caution: interchange)
M	21.7	Right on Alderman Rd
N	22.8	Continue straight. Alderman Rd becomes Maury Ave
O	23.1	Continue straight. Maury Ave becomes Jefferson Park Ave Extended
P	23.6	Right on Old Lynchburg Rd
A	24.3	Left to finish at Azalea Park

EARLYSVILLE AREA

Ride 31: Earlysville Northwest (short)

Ehart, Nortonsville

This lollipop-shaped route travels two of the author's favorite roads in northern Albemarle County. The ride is short, but it rolls along and offers spectacular views on the way out of the mountains in the southern section of Shenandoah National Park. This ride will make you want to head for the mountains to experience their beauty up close.

DISTANCE 13.3 miles

ELEVATION CHANGE 500 feet

TRAFFIC LEVEL Moderate on most roads during rush hour, but heavier on roads in and around Earlysville because many area residents commute to Charlottesville.

TERRAIN Typical rolling Blue Ridge foothills. The ride feels more uphill on the way out and more downhill on the return.

STORES ALONG THE ROUTE None.

START LOCATION Broadus Wood Elementary School. From Charlottesville, travel north on Route 29 to the Airport Road intersection. Turn left on Airport Road, left on Route 606 Dickerson Road in front of the airport, and right on Route 743 Earlysville Road, toward and through Earlysville. At the fork in the road, go left on Route 663 Buck Mountain Road. Broadus Wood Elementary School is on the left.

COMMENTS This ride is generally more scenic in the clockwise direction; however, riders looking for variety will enjoy it in either direction.

POINT	MILES	DESCRIPTION
A	0.0	Exit Broadus Wood Elementary School and turn left on Rt 663 Buck Mtn Rd
B	0.9	Bear left at Y on Rt 664 Buck Mtn Rd
C	1.3	Right on Rt 664 Markwood Rd
D	6.7	Right on Rt 663 Simmons Gap Rd
E	11.8	Right on Rt 663 Buffalo River Rd
B	12.4	Left on Rt 663 Buck Mtn Rd
A	13.3	Finish at Broadus Wood Elementary School

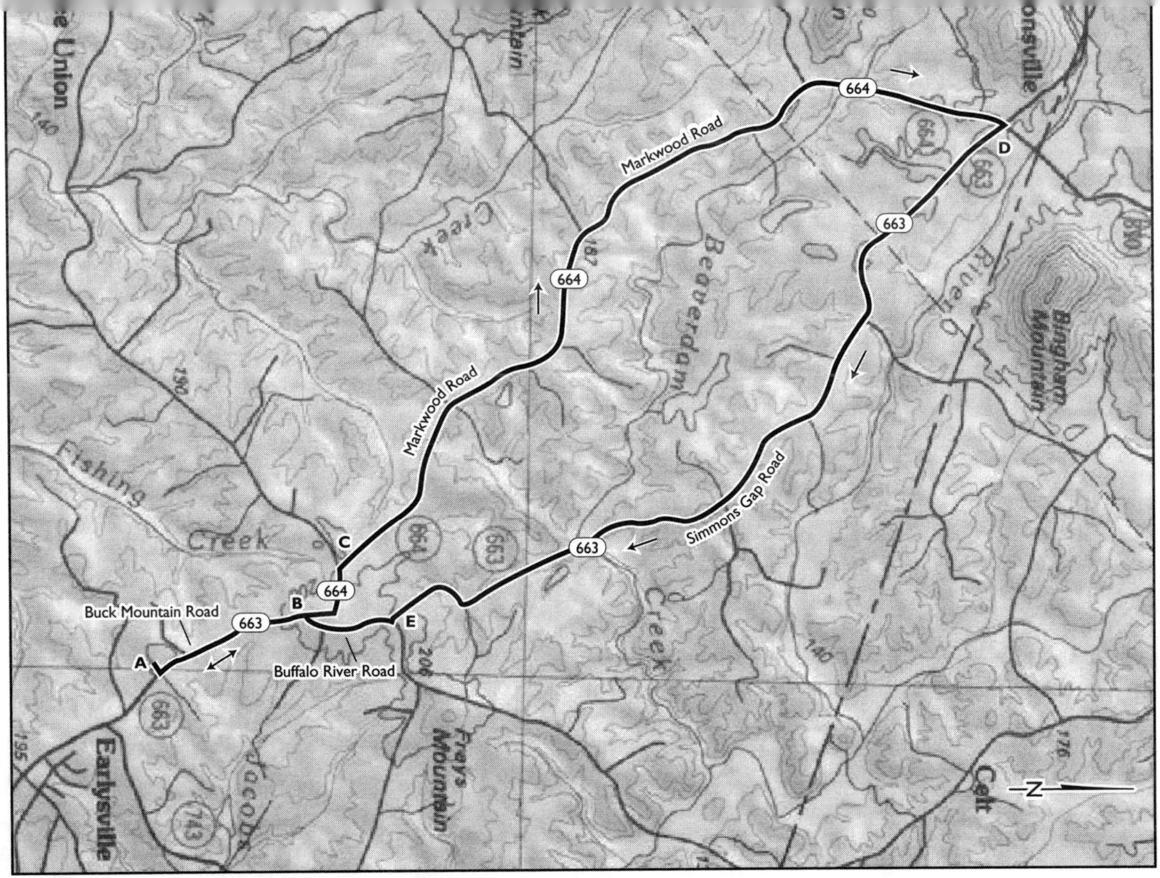

EARLYSVILLE NORTHWEST (SHORT)

Ride 32: Earlysville Northwest (long)

Free Union, Boonesville, Nortonsville

Explore scenic northwest Albemarle County along the eastern edge of the Blue Ridge Mountains and ride right up to the base of those mountains. Ride through local towns like Free Union, Boonesville, and Nortonsville. Riders will experience mostly open, rolling countryside with farms and subdivisions.

DISTANCE 23.7 miles

ELEVATION CHANGE 1,000 feet

TRAFFIC LEVEL Moderate on most roads during rush hour, but heavier on roads in and around Earlysville because many area residents commute to Charlottesville.

TERRAIN Typical rolling Blue Ridge foothills with a fun false flat downhill section on Buck Mountain Road. The ride feels more uphill on the way out to Boonesville and more downhill on the return from Nortonsville.

STORES ALONG THE ROUTE One, in Free Union at the intersection of Route 665 Buck Mountain Road and Route 601 Free Union Road.

START LOCATION Broadus Wood Elementary School. From Charlottesville, travel north on Route 29 to the Airport Road intersection. Turn left on Airport Road, left on Route 606 Dickerson Road in front of the airport, and right on Route 743 Earlysville Road, toward and through Earlysville. At the fork in the road, go left on Route 663 Buck Mountain Road. Broadus Wood Elementary School is on the left.

COMMENTS This ride can be combined with others from Earlysville to make a longer loop, and it is fun in either direction. Locals commonly ride this loop in reverse and then join the Earlysville West route at Boonesville (point E on both routes).

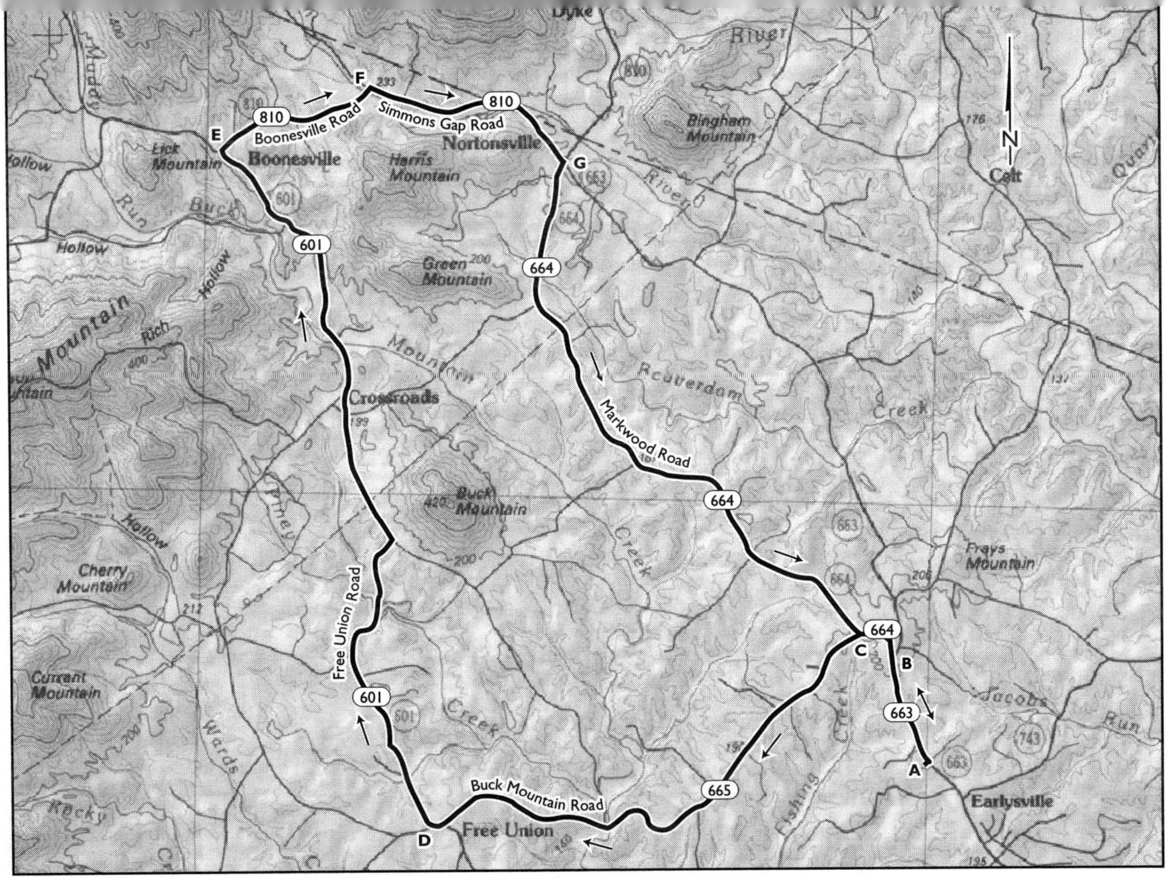

EARLYSVILLE NORTHWEST (LONG)

Ride 32: Earlysville Northwest (long)

POINT	MILES	DESCRIPTION
A	0.0	Exit Broadus Wood Elementary School and turn left on Rt 663 Buck Mtn Rd
B	0.9	Bear left at Y on Rt 664 Buck Mtn Rd
C	1.3	Continue straight on Rt 665 Buck Mtn Rd
D	6.1	Right on Rt 601 Free Union Rd. Store to the left here
—	6.2	Bear right on Rt 601 Free Union Rd
E	13.2	Right on Rt 810 Boonesville Rd
F	14.7	Bear right on Rt 810. Boonesville Rd becomes Simmons Gap Rd
G	16.7	Right on Rt 664 Markwood Rd
C	22.4	Left on Rt 664 Buck Mtn Rd
B	22.8	Straight on Rt 663 Buck Mtn Rd
A	23.7	Finish at Broadus Wood Elementary School

Ride 33: Earlysville South

Free Union, Rivanna Reservoir

A popular, fast group ride traverses this route weekly from a slightly different starting point, but you can enjoy the same ride at a more mellow pace. Along the way, you'll see sweeping views of the Blue Ridge Mountains from Buck Mountain Road. Near the ride's end, cross the peaceful Rivanna Reservoir. You can tell how much it has rained recently by looking at its color: the water is muddy in the days following a storm.

DISTANCE 22.8 miles

ELEVATION CHANGE 1,050 feet

TRAFFIC LEVEL Moderate on most roads during rush hour, but heavier on roads in and around Earlysville because many area residents commute to Charlottesville.

TERRAIN Typical rolling Albemarle County terrain featuring four climbs of roughly 200 feet elevation gain each. Done in the direction described here, you will travel down the steeper sides of the hills and up the more gradual sides.

STORES ALONG THE ROUTE One, in Free Union near the intersection of Route 665 Buck Mountain Road and Route 601 Free Union Road.

START LOCATION Broadus Wood Elementary School. From Charlottesville, travel north on Route 29 to the Airport Road intersection. Turn left on Airport Road, left on Route 606 Dickerson Road in front of the airport, and right on Route 743 Earlysville Road, toward and through Earlysville. At the fork in the road, go left on Route 663 Buck Mountain Road. Broadus Wood Elementary School is on the left.

COMMENTS A popular group ride follows the same route but starts from the intersection of Route 743 Earlysville Road and Route 660 Reas Ford Road/Earlysville Forest Road (point G). This makes the last climb as described in this ride the first one on the group ride. But the ride also can be enjoyed in the opposite direction with longer downhills and steeper climbs.

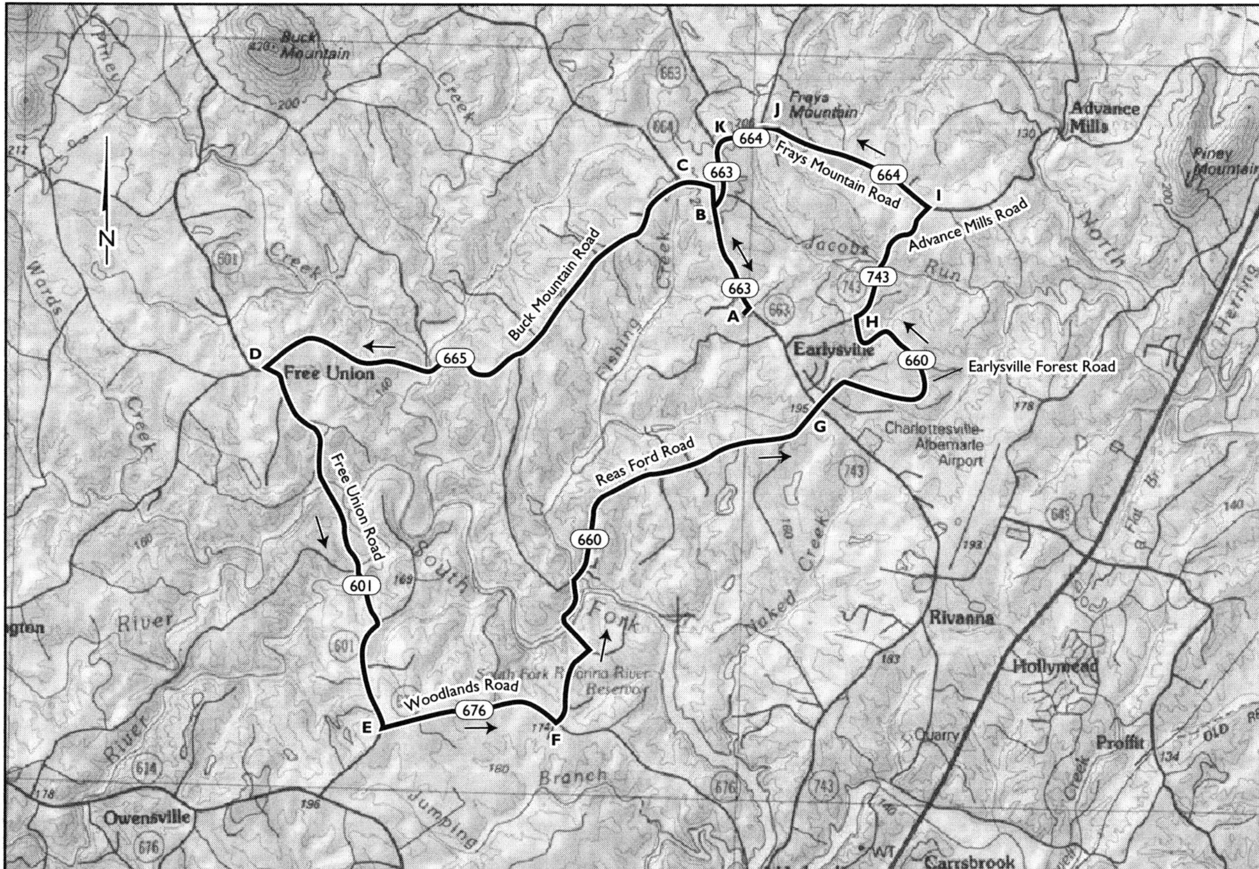

Buck Mountain
Advance Mills
Piney Mountain
Frays Mountain
Frays Mountain Road
Advance Mills Road
Buck Mountain Road
Earlysville
Earlysville Forest Road
Free Union
Free Union Road
Reas Ford Road
Charlottesville-Albemarle Airport
Woodlands Road
South Fork Rivanna River Reservoir
Rivanna
Hollymead
Profit
Quarry
Owensville
Carrsbrook
A
B
C
D
E
F
G
H
I
J
K
N

Ride 33: Earlysville South

POINT	MILES	DESCRIPTION
A	0.0	Exit Broadus Wood Elementary School and turn left on Rt 663 Buck Mtn Rd
B	0.9	Bear left at Y on Rt 664 Buck Mtn Rd
C	1.3	Continue straight on Rt 665 Buck Mtn Rd
D	6.1	Left on Rt 601 Free Union Rd. Store just past this intersection
E	9.7	Left on Rt 676 Woodlands Rd
F	11.3	Left on Rt 660 Reas Ford Rd
—	12.4	Cross Rivanna Reservoir
G	15.7	Cross Rt 743 Earlysville Rd. Rt 660 Reas Ford Rd becomes Rt 660 Earlysville Forest Rd
H	17.9	Right on Rt 743 Advance Mills Rd
I	19.1	Left on Rt 664 Frays Mtn Rd
J	20.9	Left on Rt 664 Buffalo River Rd
K	21.3	Continue straight on Rt 663 Simmons Gap Rd
B	21.9	Left on Rt 663 Buck Mtn Rd
A	22.8	Finish at Broadus Wood Elementary School

Ride 34: Earlysville West

Free Union, Boonesville, Mountfair, Whitehall, Owensville

This long ride features some of the best rural, western Albemarle County roads, as well as local favorite Route 810, which winds peacefully, often along a river, between the Blue Ridge Mountains and Fox Mountain and takes riders from Boonesville to Whitehall. Riders looking for an excuse for a break can take a side trip to Sugar Hollow Reservoir or a local vineyard for a tasting and picnic.

DISTANCE 40.2 miles

ELEVATION CHANGE 1,850 feet

TRAFFIC LEVEL Low during non-rush-hour times. Moderate on roads close to Earlysville and Free Union during rush hour because many area residents commute to Charlottesville.

TERRAIN Rolling. No one hill is huge, but the cumulative effect of so many takes its toll over the distance.

STORES ALONG THE ROUTE Two just past halfway in White Hall, and two near the end in Earlysville.

START LOCATION Broadus Wood Elementary School. From Charlottesville, travel north on Route 29 to the Airport Road intersection. Turn left on Airport Road, left on Route 606 Dickerson Road in front of the airport, and right on Route 743 Earlysville Road, toward and through Earlysville. At the fork in the road, go left on Route 663 Buck Mountain Road. Broadus Wood Elementary School is on the left.

COMMENTS This set of roads comprises one of Charlottesville's favorite long rides. Combine this ride with the Earlysville Northwest (long) ride by first doing that one in reverse and then joining this one at Boonesville (point E on both routes). The distance is slightly longer. As a second option, combine this ride with the Charlottesville Northwest ride for a 50-mile route. To do so, head north on Route 676/601 Free Union Road (point J on the Charlottesville Northwest route) toward Free Union to connect to point D on this route.

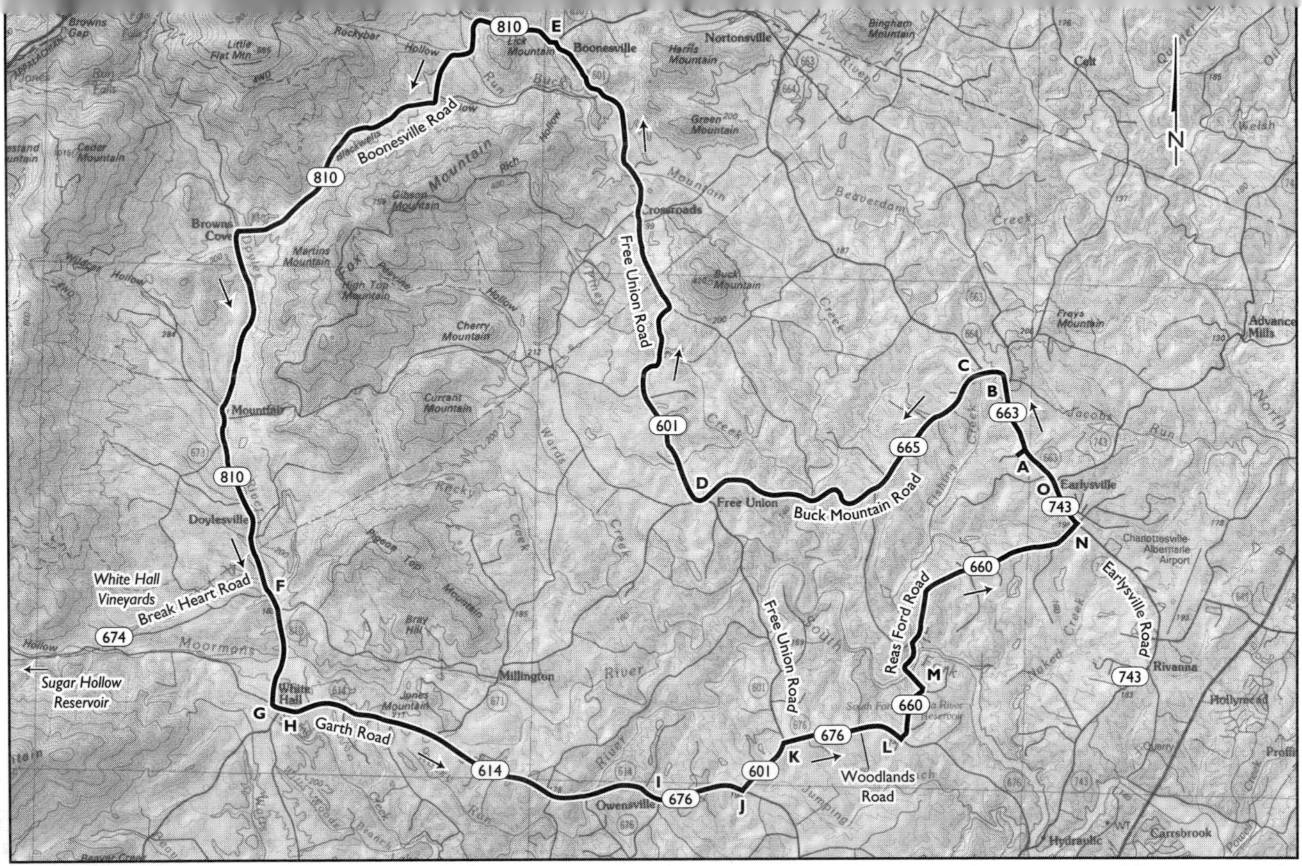

EARLYSVILLE WEST

Ride 34: Earlysville West

POINT	MILES	DESCRIPTION
A	0.0	Exit Broadus Wood Elementary School and turn left on Rt 663 Buck Mtn Rd
B	0.9	Bear left at Y on Rt 664 Buck Mtn Rd
C	1.3	Continue straight on Rt 665 Buck Mtn Rd
D	6.1	Right on Rt 601 Free Union Rd. Store to the left
—	6.2	Bear right, continuing on Rt 601 Free Union Rd (becomes Boonesville Ridge Rd)
E	13.2	Left on Rt 810 Boonesville Rd. Road will wind around for about 12 miles. When in doubt, stay on Rt 810 and do not turn onto any dirt roads
F	24.0	Continue straight. To visit White Hall Vineyards, turn right on Rt 674 Break Heart Rd (approximately one mile extra each way)
G	25.5	Bear left continuing on Rt 810 Browns Gap Turnpike. Turn right here for an out and back to Sugar Hollow Reservoir (approximately five miles extra each way). Store here
H	25.6	Continue straight on Rt 614 Garth Rd. Join 1976 Bikecentennial route here. Store here
I	31.0	Continue straight. Rt 614 Garth Rd becomes Rt 676 Garth Rd
J	32.1	Left on Rt 601 Free Union Rd
K	33.0	Right on Rt 676 Woodlands Rd
L	34.6	Left on Rt 660 Reas Ford Rd
M	35.7	Cross Rivanna Reservoir Bridge
N	39.0	Left on Rt 743 Earlysville Rd. Store here
O	39.7	Bear left on Rt 663 Buck Mtn Rd. Store here
A	40.2	Finish at Broadus Wood Elementary School

Ride 35: Earlysville Northeast

Advanced Mills, Midway, Frays Mountain

Tackle rolling hills on this route shaped like a stick with a lollipop on either end. Riders pass twice through Advance Mills, which is known for its metal truss bridge with wooden planking. On the return trip toward Advanced Mills, enjoy panoramic views of the Blue Ridge Mountains.

DISTANCE 18.0 miles

ELEVATION CHANGE 865 feet

TRAFFIC LEVEL Moderate on most roads during rush hour, but heavier on roads in and around Earlysville because many area residents commute to Charlottesville.

TERRAIN Typical rolling Blue Ridge foothills.

STORES ALONG THE ROUTE One, within the first mile.

START LOCATION Broadus Wood Elementary School. From Charlottesville, travel north on Route 29 to the Airport Road intersection. Turn left on Airport Road, left on Route 606 Dickerson Road in front of the airport, and right on Route 743 Earlysville Road, toward and through Earlysville. At the fork in the road, go left on Route 663 Buck Mountain Road. Broadus Wood Elementary School is on the left.

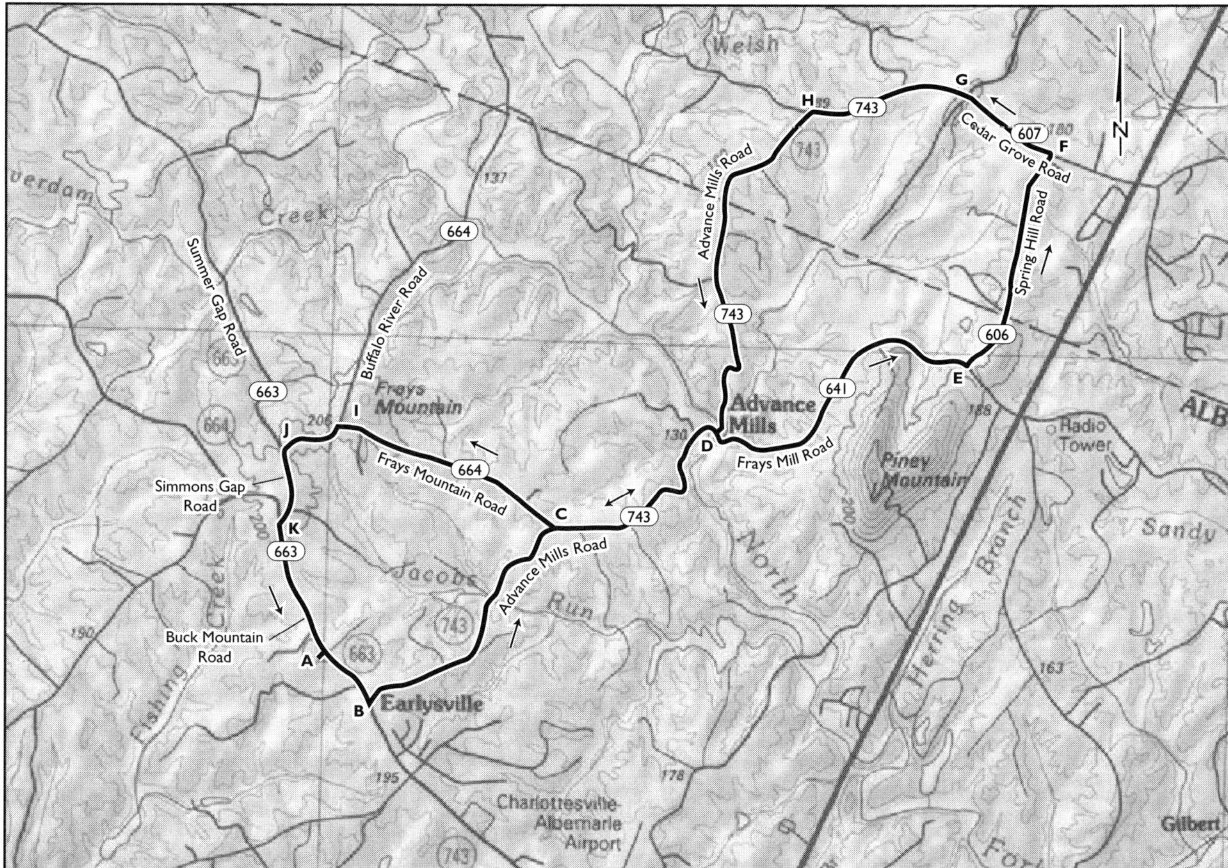

Welsh
G
H
743
607
F
Cedar Grove Road
Advance Mills Road
Spring Hill Road
Creek
664
Summer Gap Road
Buffalo River Road
743
606
663
Frays Mountain
641
E
Advance Mills
I
J
D
Frays Mill Road
Radio Tower
664
Piney Mountain
Frays Mountain Road
Simmons Gap Road
C
743
K
663
Advance Mills Road
Sandy
North
Jacobs
Run
Herring Branch
Buck Mountain Road
743
663
A
B
Earlysville
Charlottesville-Albemarle Airport
Gilbert
Fork

Ride 35: Earlysville Northeast

POINT	MILES	DESCRIPTION
A	0.0	Exit Broadus Wood Elementary School and turn right on Rt 663 Buck Mtn Rd
B	0.5	Sharp left on Rt 743 Advance Mills Rd
C	2.4	Continue straight on Rt 743 Advance Mills Rd
D	3.9	Cross metal bridge with wood planking
—	4.0	Right on Rt 641 Frays Mill Rd and cross one-lane wooden bridge
E	6.4	Left on Rt 606 Spring Hill Rd
F	8.1	Left on Rt 607 Cedar Grove Rd
G	8.8	Straight on Rt 743 Advance Mills Rd
H	10.0	Bear left on Rt 743 Advance Mills Rd
D	12.7	Bear right on Rt 743 Advance Mills Rd
—	12.8	Cross metal bridge with wood planking
C	14.3	Right on Rt 664 Frays Mtn Rd
I	16.1	Left on Rt 664 Buffalo River Rd
J	16.5	Straight on Rt 663 Simmons Gap Rd
K	17.1	Left on Rt 663 Buck Mtn Rd
A	18.0	Finish at Broadus Wood Elementary School

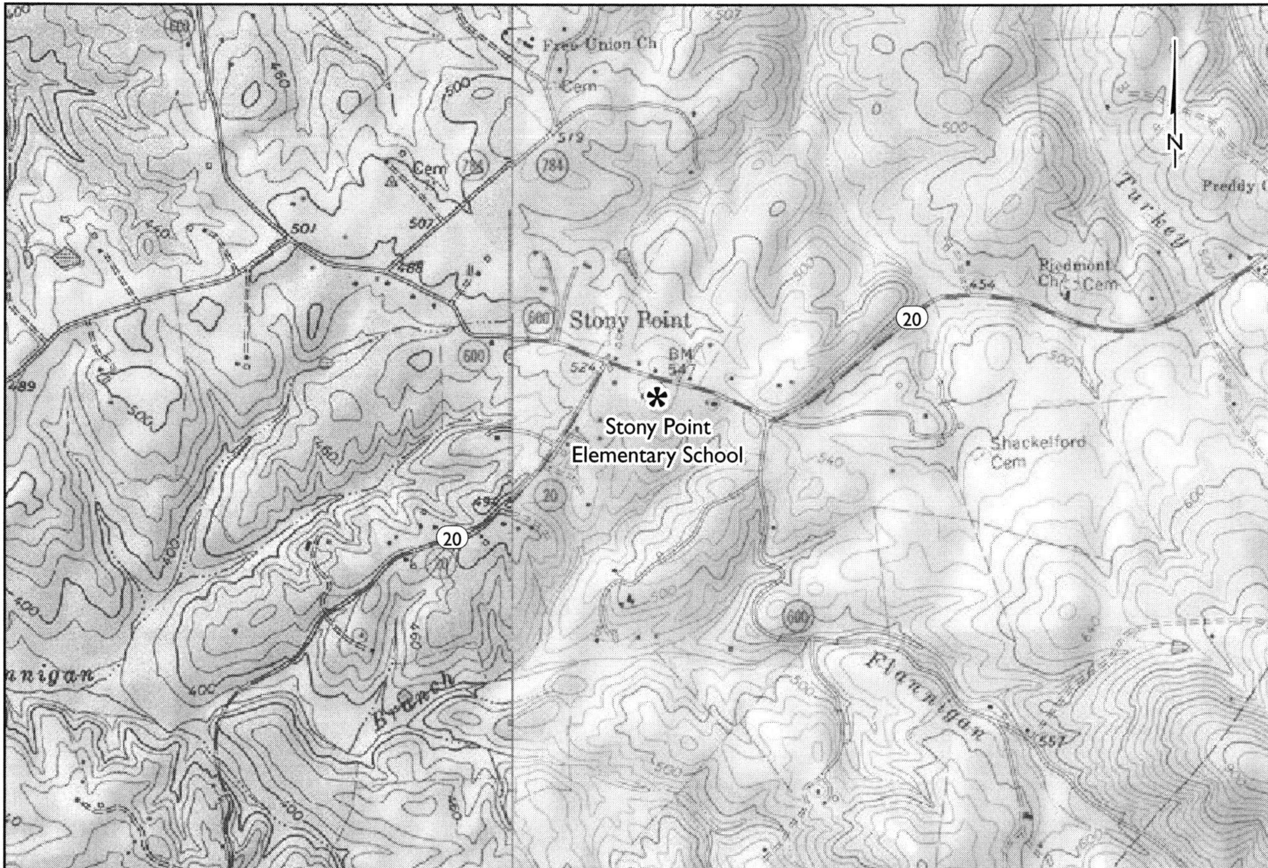

Stony Point
Elementary School
Stony Point
Shackelford Cem
Free Union Ch
Cem
Piedmont Ch Cem
Flannigan
Branch
Turkey
20
600
784
N

Ride 36: Stony Point

Burnley

This pleasant loop near the base of the Southwest Mountains gives a tour of northeastern Albemarle County near the border with Orange County. The ride features some low-traffic, narrow, twisty, well-shaded roads. Expect plenty of rolling hills. After crossing a one-lane wooden railroad bridge, it's only a little farther until riders must decide whether to stop at a local vineyard or head directly to the finish.

DISTANCE 18.7 miles

ELEVATION CHANGE 885 feet

TRAFFIC LEVEL Low, except on Route 20 Stony Point Road, which may carry moderate to heavy traffic during rush hour.

TERRAIN Typical rolling Blue Ridge foothills.

STORES ALONG THE ROUTE One, near the end.

START LOCATION Stony Point Elementary School. Take 250 East from downtown Charlottesville toward Pantops. Turn left onto Route 20 North. Follow Route 20 North approximately eight miles and turn right onto Stony Point Road. Stony Point Elementary School is on the right.

COMMENTS Route 20 is agreeable to ride during non-peak-traffic hours, but riders have the option of backtracking at any point if they are uncomfortable with the traffic. The ride is routed in this direction to minimize time spent on Route 20, which is mostly downhill and has a small shoulder in portions. Riders who enjoy gravel roads may turn right on Route 640 near the midpoint of the ride and right again on Route 784 Gilbert Station Road for an alternate route.

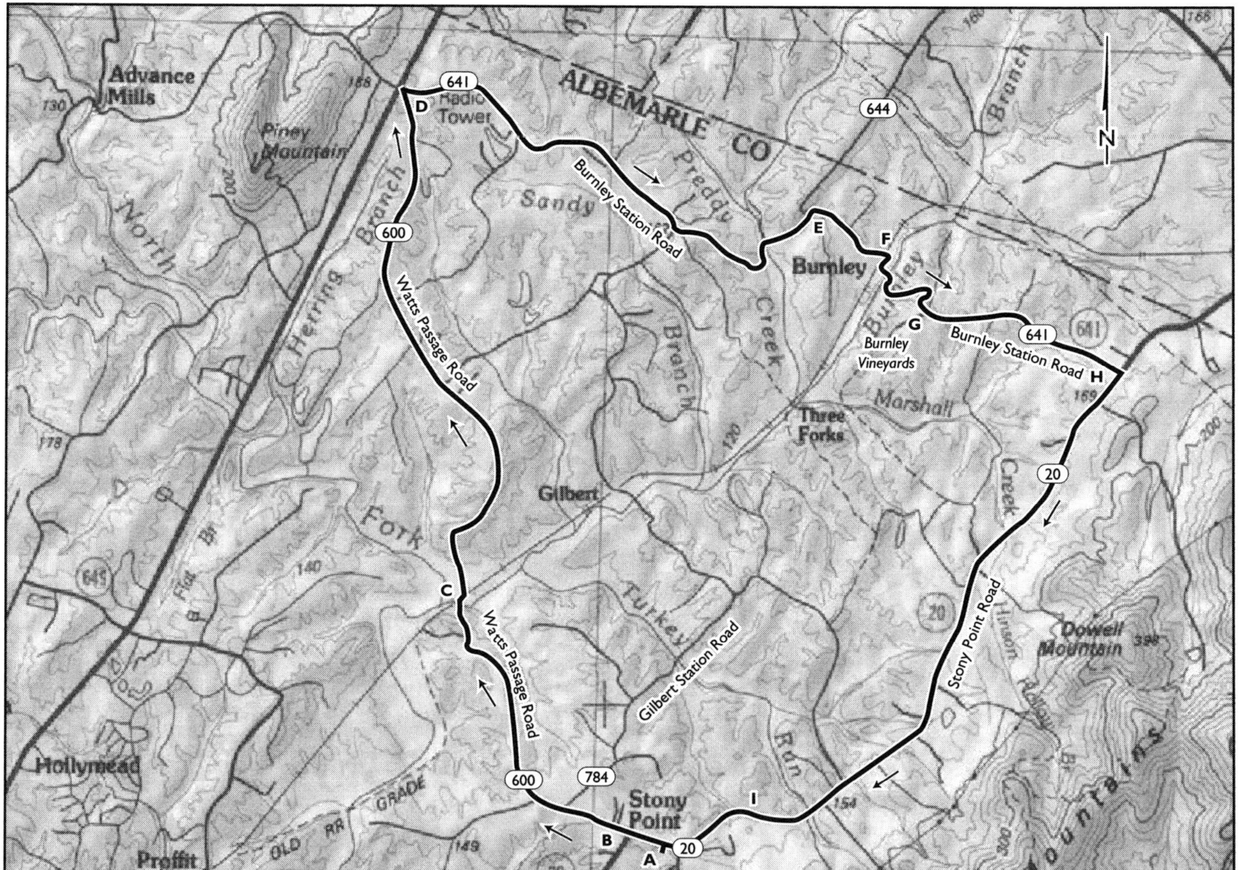

Advance Mills
Piney Mountain
Radio Tower
D
641
ALBEMARLE CO
644
N
North
Branch
600
Sandy
Burnley Station Road
Preddy
E
F
Burnley
Creek
Herring
Watts Passage Road
Branch
G
Burnley Vineyards
641
Burnley Station Road
H
Marshall
Three Forks
Gilbert
Fork
20
Creek
C
Turkey
Gilbert Station Road
Stony Point Road
Dowell Mountain
Hinson
Watts Passage Road
Run
Hollymead
600
784
Stony Point
OLD RR GRADE
I
B
A
20
Proffit
Mountains

Ride 36: Stony Point

POINT	MILES	DESCRIPTION
A	0.0	Exit Stony Point Elementary School turning left on Rt 20 Stony Point Rd
B	0.1	Continue straight on Rt 600 Watts Passage Rd. Road winds around for the next six miles. When in doubt, stay on Rt 600 Watts Passage Rd. Pass roads like Rt 784 and Rt 700 turning off
C	2.6	Continue straight on Rt 600 Watts Passage Rd crossing under railroad bridge
D	6.6	Right on Rt 641 Burnley Station Rd
E	10.5	Continue straight on Rt 641 Burnley Station Rd. Road winds around. When in doubt, stay on Rt 641 Burnley Station Rd. Rt 644 will turn off
F	11.1	Cross railroad tracks on one-lane wooden bridge
G	13.0	Continue straight. Turn right here for a side trip to Burnley Vineyards
H	13.4	Right on Rt 20 Stony Point Rd
I	17.3	Continue straight on Rt 20 Stony Point Rd. Store here
A	18.7	Finish at Stony Point Elementary School on left

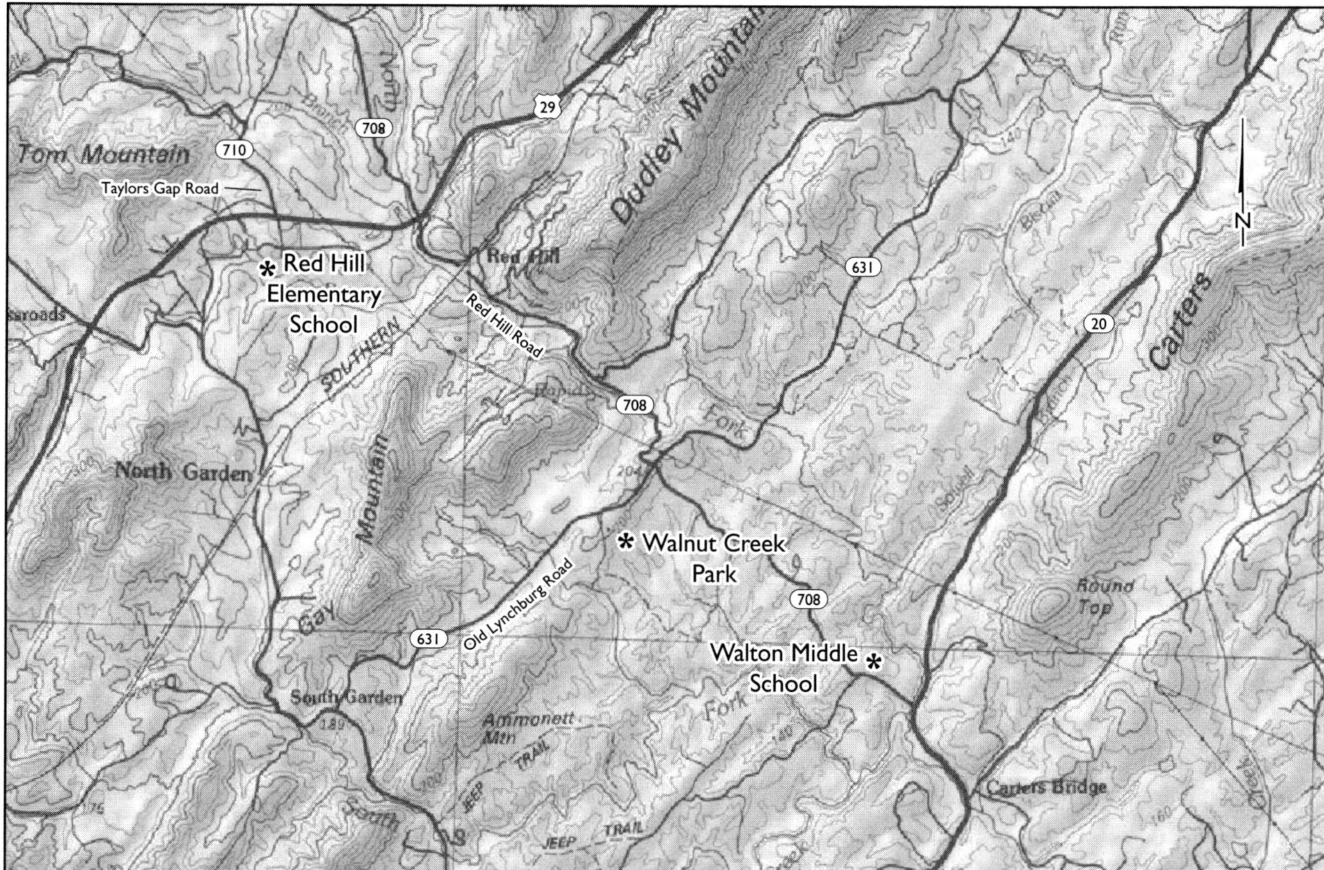

Tom Mountain
710
708
29
Taylors Gap Road
Dudley Mountain
Red Hill
Red Hill Elementary School
Red Hill Road
SOUTHERN
631
20
Carters
708
North Garden
Mountain
Walnut Creek Park
708
Round Top
Gay
631
Old Lynchburg Road
Walton Middle School
South Garden
Ammonett Mtn
Fork
JEEP TRAIL
Carters Bridge
N

Ride 37: Red Hill Northwest

Taylors Gap, Miller School, Batesville, Tom Mountain

This route highlights some of the best roads for riding in central Albemarle County, including local favorite Edge Valley Road. The ride also passes through the outskirts of Batesville, a small, historic town known for community events like the annual Apple Butter Festival.

DISTANCE 18.4 miles

ELEVATION CHANGE 1,325 feet

TRAFFIC LEVEL Low, although traffic near subdivisions on Route 637 Dick Woods Road will be heavier during rush hour, and you may encounter higher-speed traffic on the long, straight sections of Route 692 Plank Road.

TERRAIN Typical rolling Albemarle County terrain with a few short, steep climbs and one long, steady climb beginning just before mile 12.

STORES ALONG THE ROUTE One, in Batesville on Route 692 Plank Road, not far from the intersection with Route 635 Miller School Road.

START LOCATION Red Hill Elementary School. From Charlottesville, head south on Route 29. Turn left (east) at Route 710 Taylors Gap Road. Go 0.2 miles into Red Hill Elementary School parking lot.

COMMENTS This ride can be combined with the Red Hill Southeast ride. To do so, do this route first and continue straight on Route 692 Plank Road to join the other route (point H on this route; point D on that route). Or start the other ride first and join this one at Route 708 Taylors Gap Road (point D on this route; point K on that route). Expert riders can do the route from Charlottesville by generally heading out of town following the Charlottesville South ride and staying on Route 708 Red Hill Road until it crosses Route 29 and intersects this ride at point D.

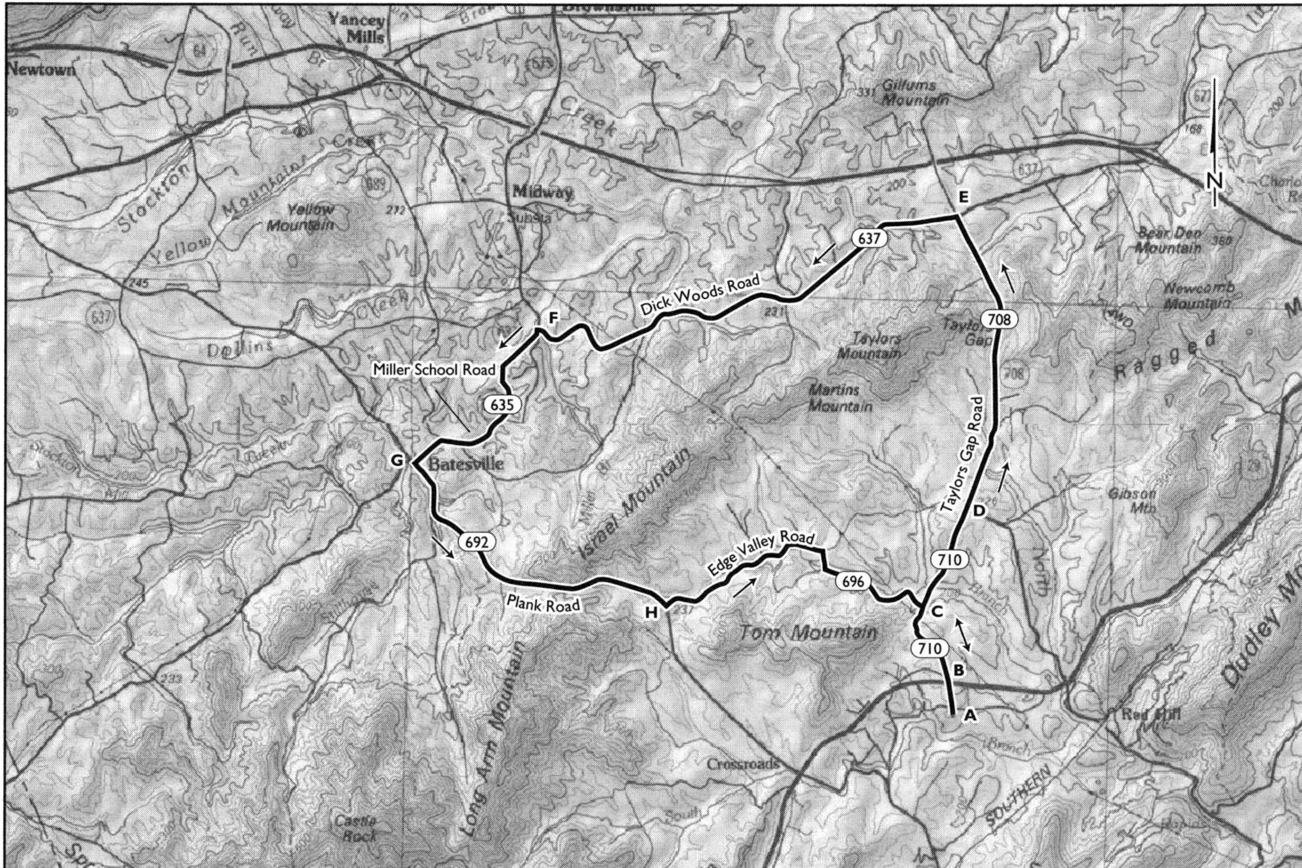

Yancey Mills
Newtown
Gilfums Mountain
Creek
Stockton
Mountain
Yellow Mountain
Yellow
Midway
Dick Woods Road
Dellins
Miller School Road
Batesville
Israel Mountain
Taylors Mountain
Taylors Gap
Martins Mountain
Ragged
Bear Den Mountain
Newcomb Mountain
Taylors Gap Road
Gibson Mtn
Edge Valley Road
Plank Road
Tom Mountain
Dudley Mou
Red Hill
Long Arm Mountain
Crossroads
Castle Rock
SOUTHERN
A
B
C
D
E
F
G
H
710
708
637
635
692
696
N

Ride 37: Red Hill Northwest

POINT	MILES	DESCRIPTION
A	0.0	Exit Red Hill Elementary School parking lot straight onto Rt 710 Taylors Gap Rd
B	0.2	Cross Rt 29 Monacan Trail. Caution: Busy road
C	1.0	Continue straight on Rt 710 Taylors Gap Rd
D	2.1	Continue straight on Rt 708 Taylors Gap Rd
E	4.8	Left on Rt 637 Dick Woods Rd
F	9.4	Left on Rt 635 Miller School Rd
G	11.5	Left on Rt 692 Plank Rd. Store about 0.1 miles to right
H	14.5	Left on Rt 696 Edge Valley Rd
C	17.3	Right on Rt 710 Taylors Gap Rd
B	18.2	Cross Rt 29 Monacan Trail. Caution: Busy road
A	18.4	Finish at Red Hill Elementary School

Ride 38: Red Hill Southeast

South Garden, North Garden, Crossroads, Tom Mountain

Ride on local favorite roads through North and South Garden and pass by Walnut Creek Park, where you can swim or mountain bike. You will pass through terrain ranging from fairly level farmland and pastures to wooded hillsides.

DISTANCE 20.8 miles

ELEVATION CHANGE 1,175 feet

TRAFFIC LEVEL Generally low on the west side of Route 29 except for Route 692 Plank Road. You may find faster or more frequent traffic there and on the east side of Route 29, in particular on Route 631 Old Lynchburg Road.

TERRAIN Typical rolling Albemarle County terrain with a few steeper climbs and descents mixed in.

STORES ALONG THE ROUTE One, in Crossroads at the intersection of Route 29 Monacan Trail and Route 692 Plank Road.

START LOCATION Red Hill Elementary School. From Charlottesville, head south on Route 29. Turn left (east) at Route 710 Taylors Gap Road. Go 0.2 miles into Red Hill Elementary School parking lot.

COMMENTS This ride can be combined with the Red Hill Northwest ride. To do so, do this route first and continue right on Route 708 Taylors Gap Road (point K on this route; point D on that route). Or start the other ride first and join this one at Route 692 Plank Road (point D on this route; point H on that route). Expert riders can do the route from Charlottesville by generally heading out of town following the Charlottesville South ride and joining the route partway through the loop at the intersection of Route 708 Red Hill Road and Route 631 Old Lynchburg Road (point I on this route; point E on that route).

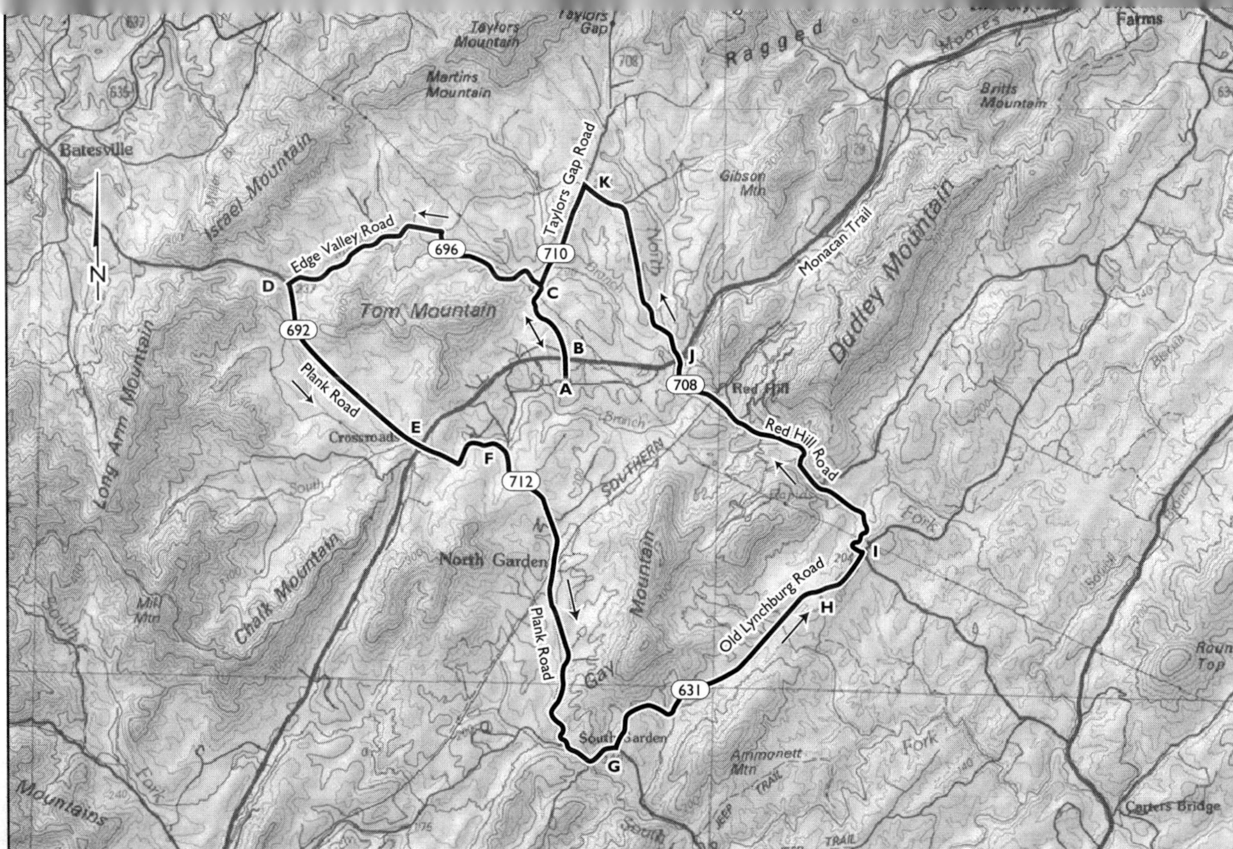

RED HILL SOUTHEAST

Ride 38: Red Hill Southeast

POINT	MILES	DESCRIPTION
A	0.0	Exit Red Hill Elementary School parking lot straight onto Rt 710 Taylors Gap Rd
B	0.2	Cross Rt 29 Monacan Trail. Caution: Busy road
C	1.0	Left on Rt 696 Edge Valley Rd
D	3.9	Left on Rt 692 Plank Rd
E	5.9	Cross Rt 29 Monacan Trail. Caution: Busy road. Store here
F	6.9	Bear right on Rt 712 Plank Rd
—	8.2	Cross under railroad tracks. Caution: One-lane passage under bridge
G	10.6	Left on Rt 631 Old Lynchburg Rd
H	13.3	Pass Walnut Creek Park entrance
I	13.8	Left on Rt 708 Red Hill Rd. Caution: Steep downhill with curves
J	16.9	Cross Rt 29 Monacan Trail. Caution: Busy road
K	18.8	Left on Rt 710 Taylors Gap Rd
C	19.8	Continue straight on Rt 710 Taylors Gap Rd
B	20.6	Cross Rt 29 Monacan Trail. Caution: Busy road
A	20.8	Finish at Red Hill Elementary School

Ride 39: Walnut Creek Park

South Garden, Keene, Alberene

Take a pleasant ride through scenic, mostly wooded terrain over a route known to locals as the former course for a popular season-opening road race. Racers would ride out the stick of this lollipop-shaped route and do multiple laps around the loop before returning to the park.

DISTANCE 21.6 miles

ELEVATION CHANGE 1,575 feet

TRAFFIC LEVEL Moderate; however, Old Lynchburg Road, Route 712 Plank Road, and Route 715 Keene Road are tight and twisty and often are busier during rush hour.

TERRAIN Typical rolling Albemarle County terrain with several steep climbs and descents mixed in. There are steep half-mile or longer hills at the beginning and end.

STORES ALONG THE ROUTE One, just off the route at the intersection of Route 712 Plank Road and Route 20 in Keene.

START LOCATION Walnut Creek Park. From Charlottesville, drive south on Route 29 about six miles. Turn left on Route 708 Red Hill Road (look for brown Walnut Creek Park sign before the turn). Drive about three miles and turn right on Route 631 Old Lynchburg Road. The park is about one-half mile on the left. Turn into the entrance, drive downhill, and park at the first (cycle) lot at the bottom of the hill on the right.

COMMENTS Expert riders can do the ride from Charlottesville by generally heading out of town following the Charlottesville South ride but going straight at point E on that route and joining this route at point B, near its start at Walnut Creek Park. A per-person fee is charged for entering the park during daytime hours between Memorial Day and Labor Day. See http://www.albemarle.org for fees. Entry is free during the rest of the year and in the evenings year-round. The park is a popular destination for local mountain bikers.

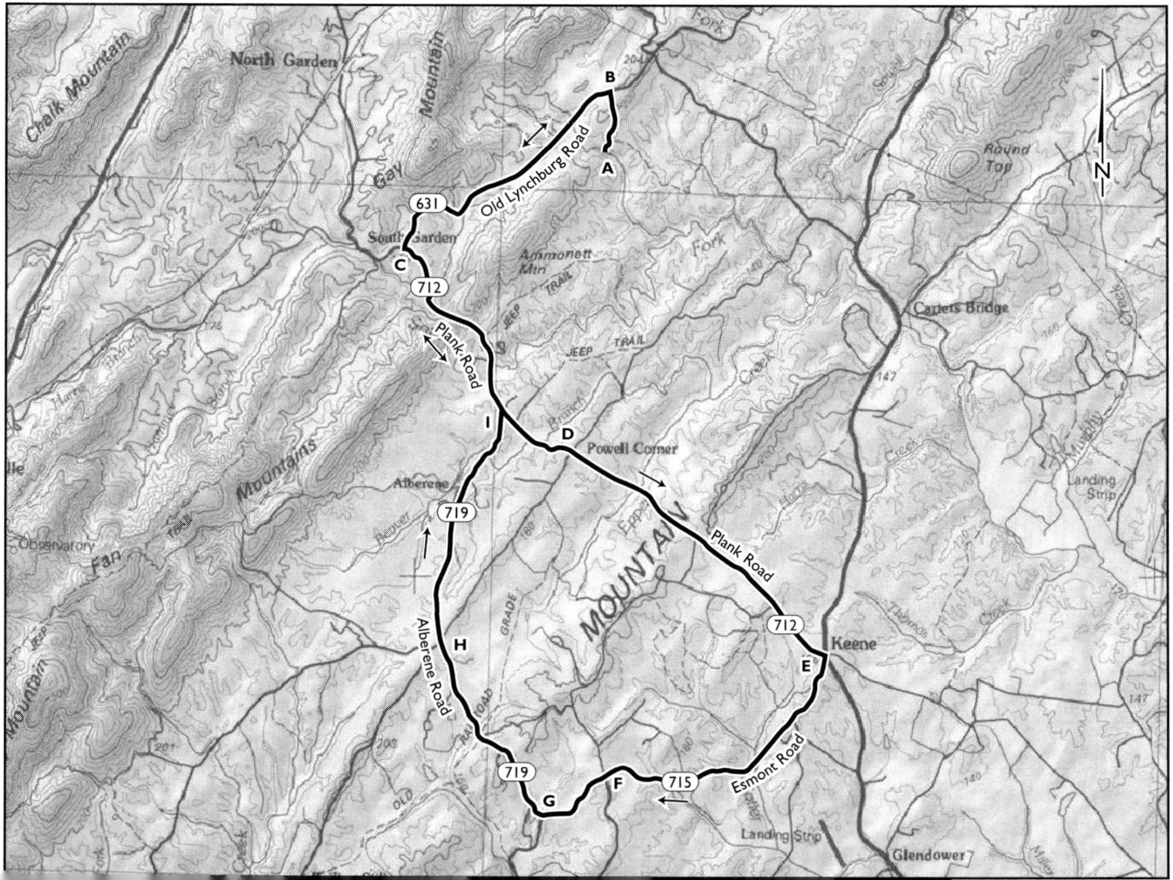
North Garden
Chalk Mountain
Gay Mountain
Old Lynchburg Road
631
South Garden
Ammonett Mtn
712
Plank Road
Powell Corner
Alberene
719
Fan Mountains
Observatory
MOUNTAIN
Alberene Road
Keene
Esmont Road
715
Landing Strip
Glendower
Carters Bridge
Round Top
A
B
C
D
E
F
G
H
I
N

Ride 39: Walnut Creek Park

POINT	MILES	DESCRIPTION
A	0.0	Left out of lower (aka cycle) parking lot at Walnut Creek Park onto entrance road
B	0.5	Left on Rt 631 Old Lynchburg Rd
C	3.2	Left on Rt 712 Plank Rd
D	5.1	Continue straight on Rt 712 Plank Rd, crossing Rt 717 Secretary Sand Rd
E	8.9	Right on Rt 715 Esmont Rd immediately before the intersection with Rt 20. Store across Rt 20
F	11.7	Continue straight on Rt 715 Esmont Rd, crossing Rt 627 Green Mtn Rd
G	12.4	Right on Rt 719 Alberene Rd
H	14.3	Continue almost straight on Rt 719 Alberene Rd, crossing Rt 717 Secretary Sand Rd
I	16.6	Left on Rt 712 Plank Rd
C	18.5	Right on Rt 631 Old Lynchburg Rd
B	21.1	Right into Walnut Creek Park on entrance road
A	21.6	Right into parking lot

Ride 40: Carters Bridge

Overton, Blenheim

This ride covers much of the route of a popular regional road race that signals the start of the race season every spring. It also rolls past the famous Kluge Estate, including the newly added Kluge Vineyards, and near Ash Lawn, the home of James Monroe. Riders can complete the loop as described to cover the longer distance (16.7 miles) or take the shortcut to follow the race course exactly for about 12.5 miles. The side trip to Ash Lawn adds about two miles each way.

DISTANCE 16.7 miles

ELEVATION CHANGE 640 feet

TRAFFIC LEVEL Low to moderate overall, with fast traffic on the short sections of Route 20 Scottsville Road at either end of the ride.

TERRAIN Typical rolling Albemarle County terrain, with more climbing and descending in the first half than the second.

STORES ALONG THE ROUTE None.

START LOCATION Walton Middle School. From Charlottesville, drive south from I-64 about 7.6 miles on Route 20. Turn right on Route 708 Red Hill. Walton Middle School is on the right after 0.2 miles.

COMMENTS Route 20 Scottsville Road can be very busy at most times of the day. There is only a small shoulder, so use caution while on this road or turning on or off it. For a shorter option of about 12.5 miles, turn right on Route 727 Blenheim Road (point E) and right again on Route 708 Secretary Road (point H) to rejoin the ride.

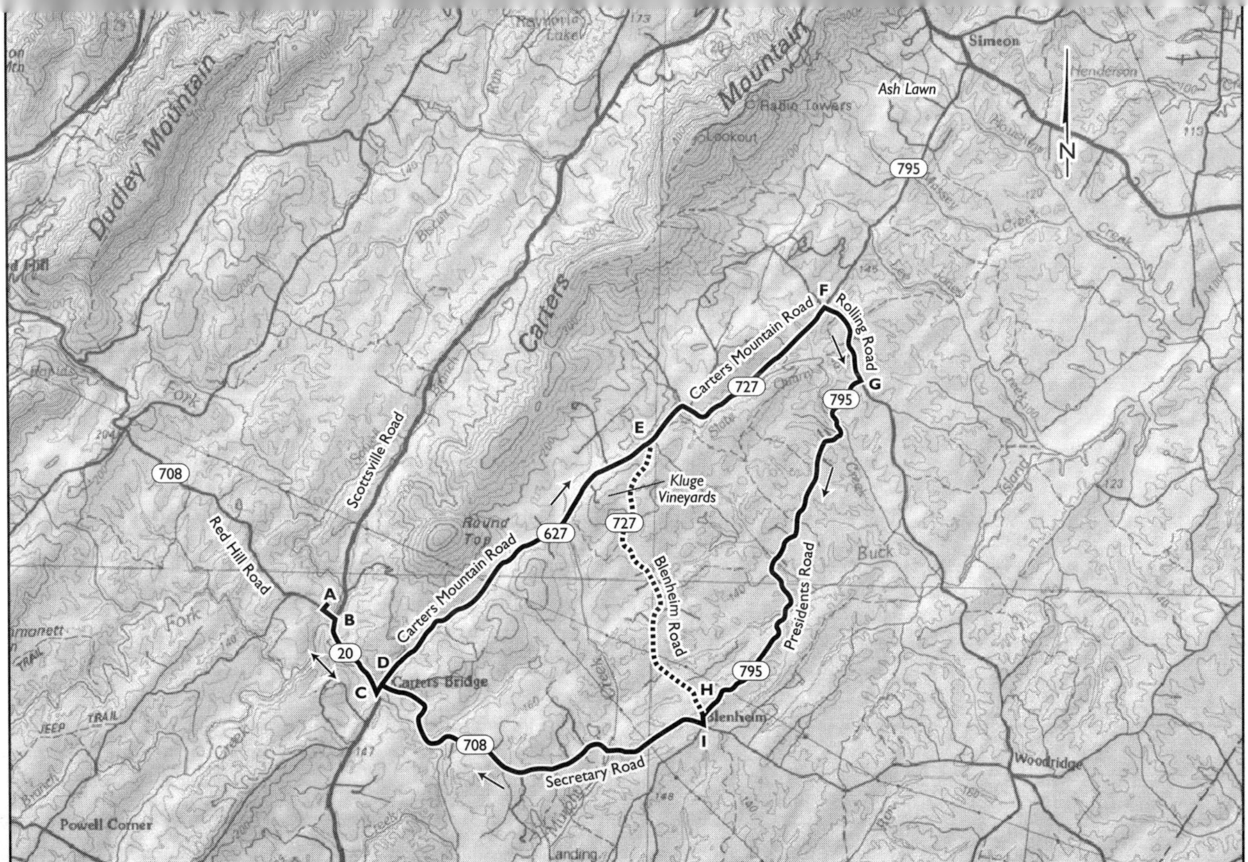

CARTERS BRIDGE

Ride 40: Carters Bridge

POINT	MILES	DESCRIPTION
A	0.0	Exit Walton Middle School parking lot and turn left on Rt 708 Red Hill Rd
B	0.2	Right on Rt 20 Scottsville Rd. Caution: Busy road
C	1.0	Left on Rt 627 Carters Mtn Rd
D	1.1	Continue straight on Rt 627 Carters Mtn Rd
E	4.6	Continue straight on Rt 627 Carters Mtn Rd. Turn right on Rt 727 Blenheim Rd to take the shortcut or visit Kluge Vineyards
F	6.2	Right on Rt 795 Rolling Rd. Briefly join the 1976 Bikecentennial route here. To visit Ash Lawn proceed straight on Rt 795 James Monroe Pkwy for an out and back extension of about two miles each way
G	7.6	Right on Rt 795 Presidents Rd
H	11.7	Left on Rt 795 Blenheim Rd. Rt 727 Blenheim Rd shortcut rejoins here
I	11.8	Right on Rt 708 Secretary Rd
D	15.6	Left on Rt 627 Carters Mtn Rd
C	15.7	Right on Rt 20 Scottsville Rd. Caution: Busy road
B	16.5	Left on Rt 708 Red Hill Rd
A	16.7	Right to finish at Walton Middle School

Ride 41: Esmont

Tapscott, Porter

This route takes you to a less-traveled and more "Southern" part of Albemarle County only a few miles from the James River. Riding through Esmont is almost like going back in time because you are far from the more developed parts of Albemarle. You won't see many cars, but you will pass through a mix of woodlands and open farmlands. Early in the ride, you can look east toward the flatter parts of Virginia. Later, you will see some evidence of logging, which is common on private lands in the southeastern United States.

DISTANCE 15.9 miles

ELEVATION CHANGE 650 feet

TRAFFIC LEVEL Low.

TERRAIN Typical rolling Albemarle County terrain. Generally, you are climbing as you head away from the James River and descending as you head toward it.

STORES ALONG THE ROUTE None, but there is one on Route 6 slightly west of the intersection with Route 627 Porters Road.

START LOCATION Simpson Park, or Benjamin Franklin Yancey Elementary School across the street. From Charlottesville, take Route 20 Scottsville Road south. At Keene, turn right on Route 712 Plank Road then left on Route 715 Esmont Road. Go left on Route 627 Porters Road. Cross Route 6 and turn right on Simpson Drive (park entrance).

COMMENTS Simpson Park offers swimming and other recreational opportunities.

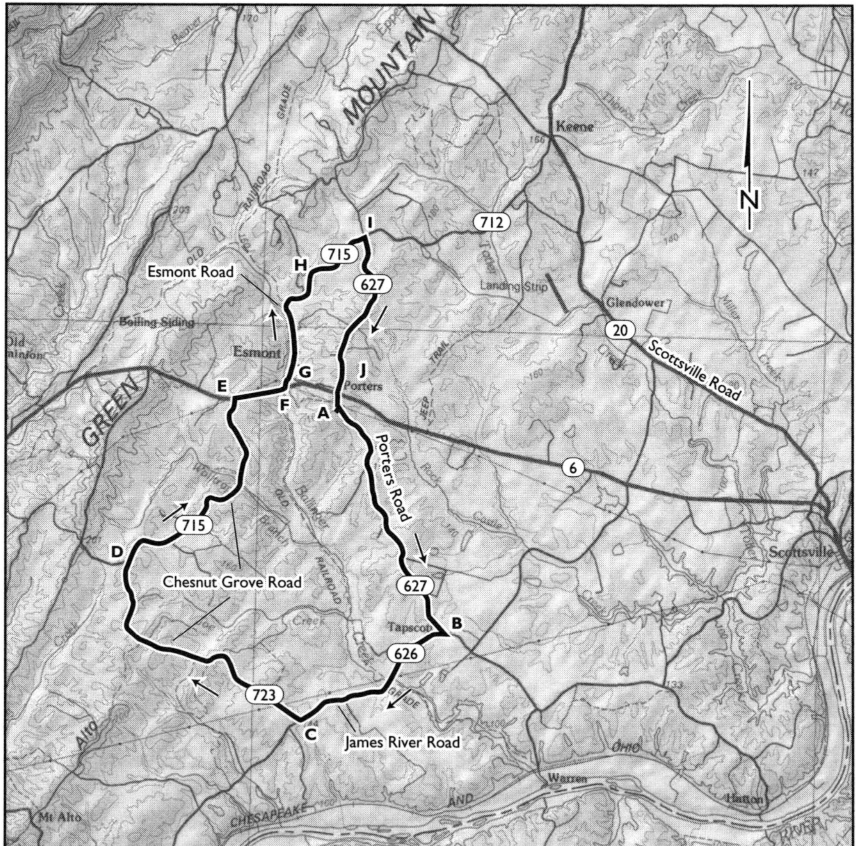
MOUNTAIN
Keene
712
I
715
H
Esmont Road
627
Landing Strip
Glendower
Boiling Siding
20
Scottsville Road
Esmont
G
J
Porters
E
F
A
GREEN
Porters Road
6
715
D
Scottsville
627
Chesnut Grove Road
Tapscot
B
626
723
C
James River Road
Warren
Hatton
Mt Alto
CHESAPEAKE
AND
OHIO
RIVER
N

ESMONT

Ride 41: Esmont

POINT	MILES	DESCRIPTION
A	0.0	Exit Simpson Park across from Yancey Elementary School and turn right on Rt 627 Porters Rd
B	2.8	Right on Rt 626 James River Rd
C	4.8	Right on Rt 723 Chesnut Grove Rd
D	8.0	Continue straight on Rt 715 Chesnut Grove Rd
E	10.8	Right on Rt 6. Caution: Busy road
F	11.4	Left on Rt 715 Esmont Rd
G	11.5	Left on Rt 715 Esmont Rd. Pages Store Rd goes straight
H	13.0	Continue straight on Rt 715 Esmont Rd
I	13.7	Right on Rt 627 Porters Rd
J	15.6	Cross Rt 6. Caution: Busy road
A	15.9	Finish at Simpson Park on the right

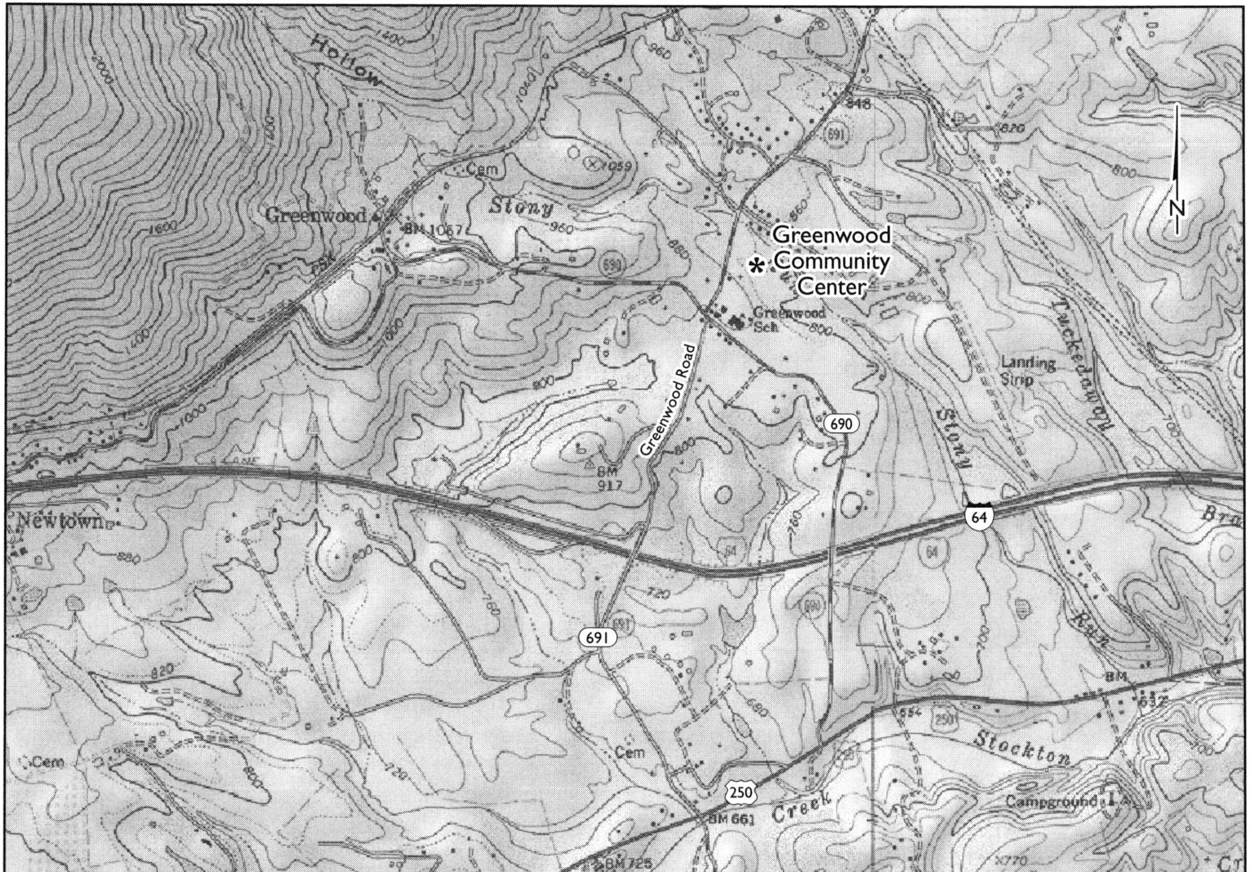
Greenwood Community Center
Greenwood Road
Greenwood
Greenwood Sch
Stony
Hollow
Cem
Newtown
Landing Strip
Tuckedaway Run
Stockton Creek
Campground
690
691
64
250
N

Ride 42: Greenwood South

Newtown

This short but sweet ride gives you a taste of the beautiful countryside of western Albemarle County at the base of the Blue Ridge Mountains. You will climb one big hill, but it occurs early in the ride and is followed by a downhill and generally rolling roads. The beginning of this ride follows the 1976 Bikecentennial route.

DISTANCE 9.3 miles

ELEVATION CHANGE 500 feet

TRAFFIC LEVEL Low, except for a 0.3-mile section on Route 250, which may have significant traffic during busy times of the day.

TERRAIN One big climb at the start, with a few steep sections followed by a long downhill and rollers.

STORES ALONG THE ROUTE None.

START LOCATION Greenwood Community Center. Take Route 250 West from Charlottesville. After passing turns for Crozet, turn right on Route 691 Greenwood Road. At the intersection with the post office, take a left on Route 690 immediately followed by a right on Route 691. Proceed 0.2 miles to Greenwood Community Center on the right.

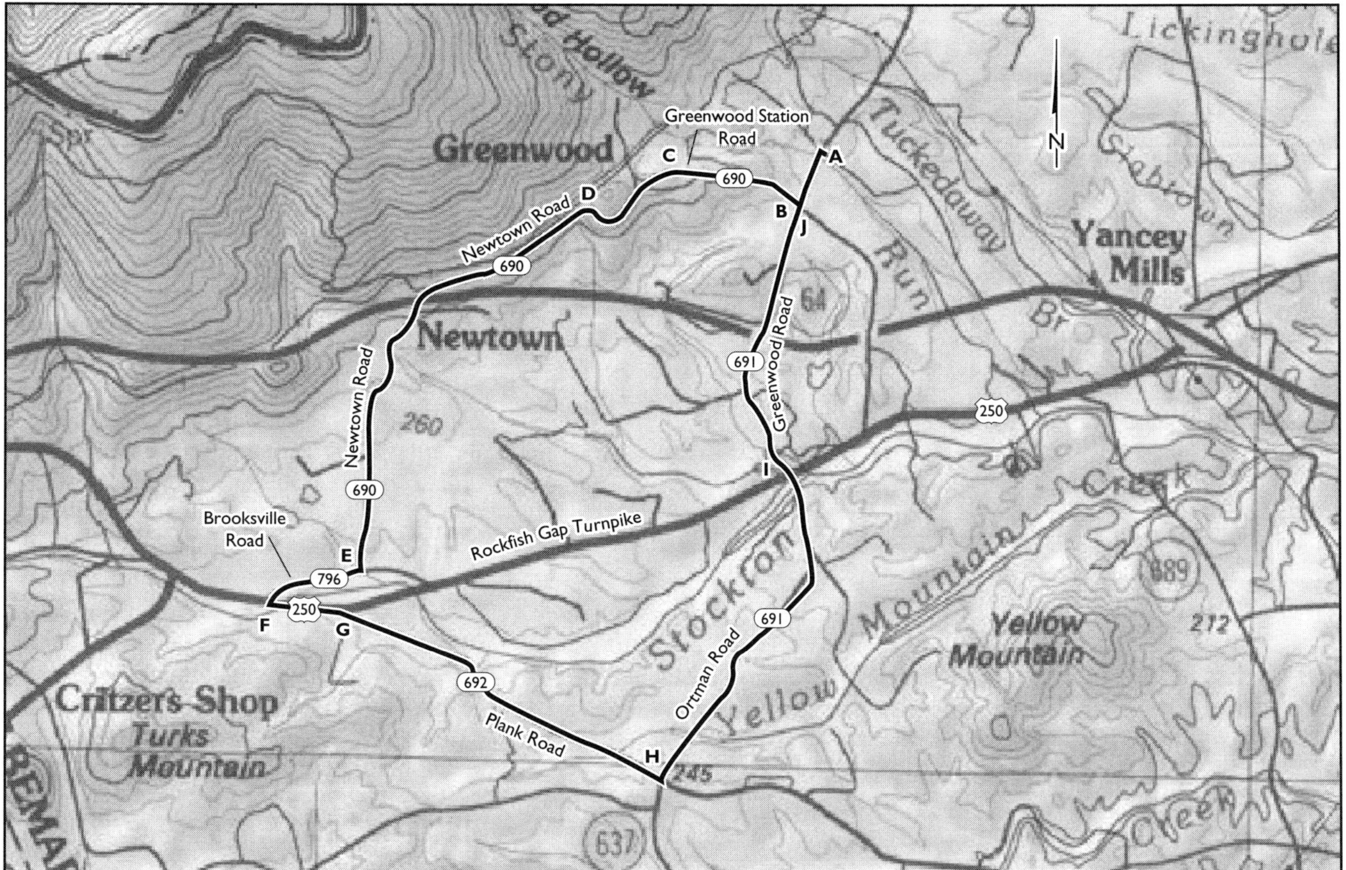
Greenwood Station Road
Greenwood
Newtown Road
Newtown
Newtown Road
Greenwood Road
Tuckedaway Run
Yancey Mills
Stony Hollow
Brooksville Road
Rockfish Gap Turnpike
Stockton
Ortman Road
Plank Road
Yellow Mountain
Mountain Creek
Critzers Shop
Turks Mountain
Lickinghole
A
B
C
D
E
F
G
H
I
J
N
690
691
692
796
250
637
689
245
212
260
64

Ride 42: Greenwood South

POINT	MILES	DESCRIPTION
A	0.0	Exit Greenwood Community Center and turn left on Rt 691 Greenwood Rd
B	0.2	Right on Rt 690 Greenwood Station Rd
C	1.0	Switchback left continuing on Rt 690 Greenwood Station Rd
D	1.5	Rt 690 Greenwood Station Rd becomes Newtown Rd
—	2.3	Cross under I-64
E	3.7	Right on Rt 796 Brooksville Rd
F	4.1	Left on Rt 250 Rockfish Gap Turnpike. Caution: Busy road
G	4.4	Right on Rt 692 Plank Rd
H	6.1	Left on Rt 691 Ortman Rd
I	7.7	Cross Rt 250 Rockfish Gap Turnpike where Rt 691 Ortman Rd becomes Greenwood Rd. Caution: Intersection is at the bottom of a steep downhill with a stop sign
—	8.4	Cross I-64 (no interchange)
J	9.0	Left on Rt 690 Greenwood Station Rd
B	9.1	Right on Rt 691 Greenwood Rd
A	9.3	Finish at Greenwood Community Center

Ride 43: Greenwood Southwest

Newtown, Afton, Avon

Are you curious to experience riding in the Blue Ridge Mountains after looking at them during so many of the other rides in this book? This ride sends you partway up the mountains on a local favorite long climb along the 1976 Bikecentennial route to Afton. You will also spend time in Albemarle and Nelson Counties and pass two vineyards, Afton Mountain and Cardinal Point, where you can break for a tour and tasting. This route is not recommended for beginners because of the two long climbs early in the ride.

DISTANCE 22.2 miles

ELEVATION CHANGE 1,465 feet

TRAFFIC LEVEL Low, except for a 0.7-mile section on Route 250 Rockfish Gap Turnpike, which may have significant traffic during busy times of the day.

TERRAIN Two big hills (the second climb gains almost 600 feet) at the beginning of the ride, followed by typical rolling Albemarle County terrain.

STORES ALONG THE ROUTE None.

START LOCATION Greenwood Community Center. Take Route 250 West from Charlottesville. After passing turns for Crozet, turn right on Route 691 Greenwood Road. At the intersection with the post office, take a left on Route 690 immediately followed by a right on Route 691. Proceed 0.2 miles to Greenwood Community Center on the right.

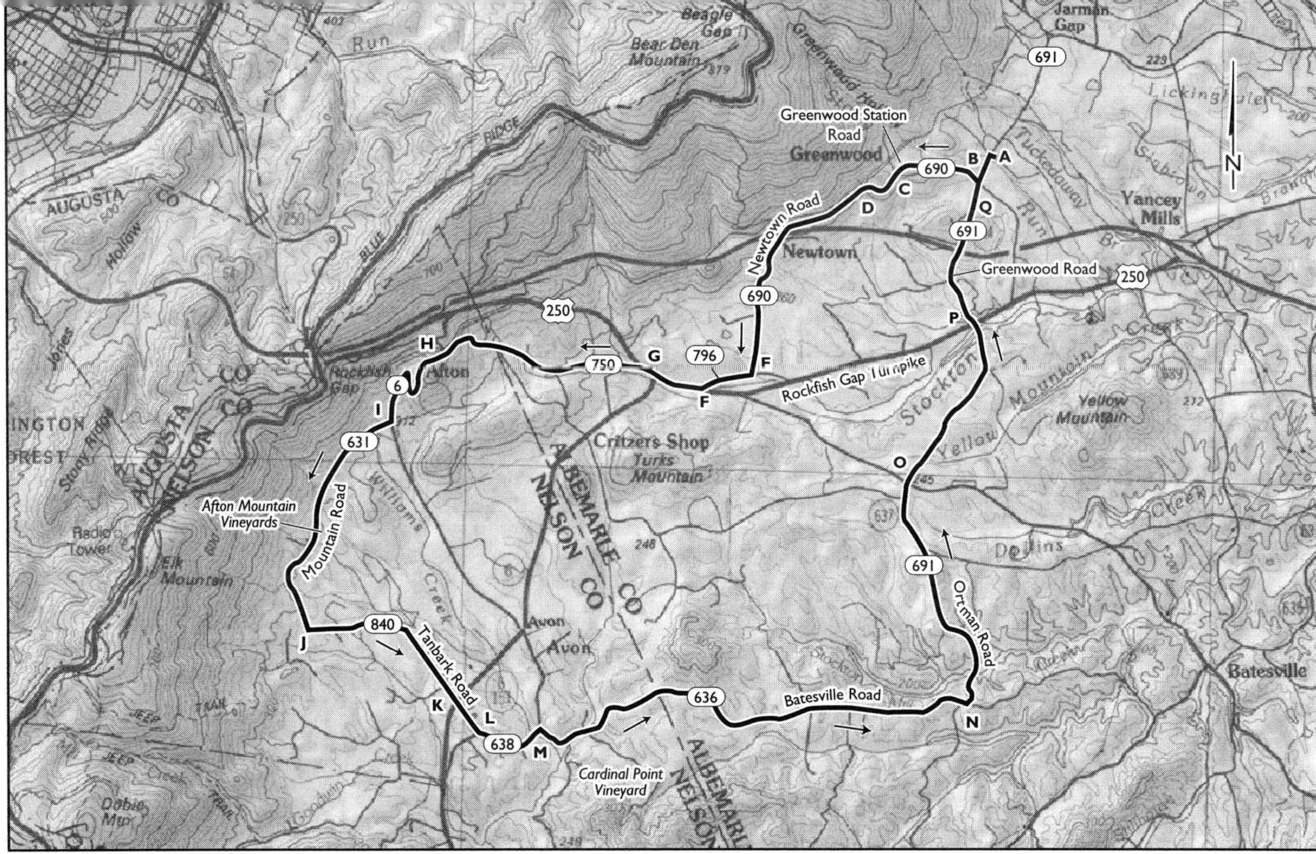

GREENWOOD SOUTHWEST

Ride 43: Greenwood Southwest

POINT	MILES	DESCRIPTION
A	0.0	Exit Greenwood Community Center and turn left on Rt 691 Greenwood Rd
B	0.2	Right on Rt 690 Greenwood Station Rd
C	1.0	Switchback left continuing on Rt 690 Greenwood Station Rd
D	1.5	Rt 690 Greenwood Station Rd becomes Newtown Rd
—	2.3	Cross under I-64
E	3.7	Right on Rt 796 Brooksville Rd
F	4.1	Right on Rt 250 Rockfish Gap Turnpike. Caution: Busy road
—	4.5	Continue straight on Rt 250 Rockfish Gap Turnpike where Rt 151 turns left
G	4.7	Left on Rt 750 Old Turnpike Rd (follow 1976 Bikecentennial route signs)
H	6.7	Left on Rt 6 Afton Mtn Rd
I	7.8	Right on Rt 631 Mtn Rd

POINT	MILES	DESCRIPTION
—	9.1	Pass Afton Mtn Vineyards on left
J	10.1	Left on Rt 840 Tanbark Rd
K	11.7	Cross Rt 151 Rockfish Valley Rd
L	12.1	Left on Rt 638 Avon Rd
M	12.6	Right on Rt 636 Batesville Rd. Road twists and turns and other roads turn off
—	13.3	Pass Cardinal Point Vineyard on right
N	16.7	Left on Rt 691 Ortman Rd
O	18.9	Cross Rt 692 Plank Rd
P	20.6	Cross Rt 250 Rockfish Gap Turnpike where Rt 691 Ortman Rd becomes Greenwood Rd. Caution: Intersection is at the bottom of a steep downhill with a stop sign
—	21.3	Cross I-64 (no interchange)
Q	21.9	Left on Rt 690 Greenwood Station Rd
B	22.0	Right on Rt 691 Greenwood Rd
A	22.2	Finish at Greenwood Community Center

Greene County

rides leaving from

Stanardsville

Ride 44: Stanardsville North

Brills Shop, South River

Greene County, a small but beautiful area north of Albemarle, is one of the gateways to Shenandoah National Park. On this ride, explore the area around Stanardsville, mostly to the northeast but also a little to the southwest. Because Stanardsville is a small town, little time is required to get to quiet country roads from the ride's start. One of the most pleasant sections of the ride is along the South River, where the terrain is relatively level and the views of the mountains are spectacular. Riders wanting fewer miles can do just one of the two loops on this route.

DISTANCE 22 miles

ELEVATION CHANGE 1,040 feet

TRAFFIC LEVEL Low to moderate throughout, except when on or crossing Routes 33, 230, and 622, which often carry more traffic, particularly during rush hour.

TERRAIN Typical rolling Blue Ridge foothills.

STORES ALONG THE ROUTE One, in Stanardsville across Business Route 33 from the school complex.

START LOCATION William Monroe High School. From Charlottesville, take Route 29 North to the intersection of Routes 29 and 33. Turn left on Route 33 West and continue for approximately six miles. Go through one stoplight. The next light will be a flashing yellow. Turn right on Celt Road. The first left will be William Monroe High School. From Elkton or Harrisonburg, take Route 33 East and turn left at the flashing yellow light (Celt Road). The first left will be William Monroe High School.

COMMENTS This ride can be 16 miles or 22 miles long with no modifications because the route heads past the start/finish point along the way. (Think of it as a figure 8.) This is a great ride to do in its entirety, or you can ride just one part if you are short on time, inclination, or fitness.

STANARDSVILLE NORTH

Ride 44: Stanardsville North

POINT	MILES	DESCRIPTION
A	0.0	Exit William Monroe High School and turn left on Rt 622 Celt Rd
B	0.2	Right on Business Rt 33 Main St, which becomes Spottswood Trail
C	2.0	Left on Old Rt 33 Spottswood Trail
D	2.6	Left on Rt 609 Fredericksburg Rd
E	5.0	Left on Rt 619 Dundee Rd
F	9.3	Left on Rt 230 Madison Rd
G	10.5	Right on Rt 621 South River Rd
H	12.5	Left on Rt 637 Octonia Rd and cross narrow bridge
I	14.3	Caution: Poor road surface
—	14.4	Right on Rt 1001 Ford Ave
J	15.8	Right on Business Rt 33 Main St
B	15.9	Left on Rt 622 Celt Rd
A	16.1	Finish at or continue past William Monroe High School
K	16.3	Cross Rt 33 Stanardsville Bypass
L	18.3	Right on Rt 624 Pea Ridge Rd
M	19.6	Right on Rt 646 Blue Run Rd
N	20.4	Right on Rt 33 Spottswood Trail (aka Stanardsville Bypass)
O	20.9	Left to cross median and continue on to Business Rt 33, which becomes Main St
B	21.8	Right on Rt 622 Celt Rd
A	22.0	Finish at William Monroe High School

Ride 45: Stanardsville South

Amicus, Geer

Experience the rolling Blue Ridge foothills in southern Greene County. Near the end of the ride, travel on Route 810, one of the most scenic roads in the region. You may well share the road with other cyclists, and you will enjoy great views of the Blue Ridge Mountains, located within Shenandoah National Park.

DISTANCE 15.6 miles

ELEVATION CHANGE 710 feet

TRAFFIC LEVEL Moderate throughout, except when on or crossing Routes 33 or 633, which often carry more traffic, particularly during rush hour.

TERRAIN Typical rolling Blue Ridge foothills with some short, steep hills in the first half.

STORES ALONG THE ROUTE One, in Stanardsville across Business Route 33 from the school complex.

START LOCATION William Monroe High School. From Charlottesville, take Route 29 North to the intersection of Routes 29 and 33. Turn left on Route 33 West and continue for approximately six miles. Go through one stoplight. The next light will be a flashing yellow. Turn right on Celt Road. The first left will be William Monroe High School. From Elkton or Harrisonburg, take Route 33 East and turn left at the flashing yellow light (Celt Road). The first left will be William Monroe High School.

COMMENTS Riders wanting to connect to Albemarle County rides can turn left (south) on Route 810 (point G) and eventually come to the intersection of Route 664 Markwood Road and Route 663 Simmons Gap Road, which is a connecting point to two of the Earlysville rides in this book (point D on the Earlysville Northwest [short] route; point G on the Earlysville Northwest [long] route).

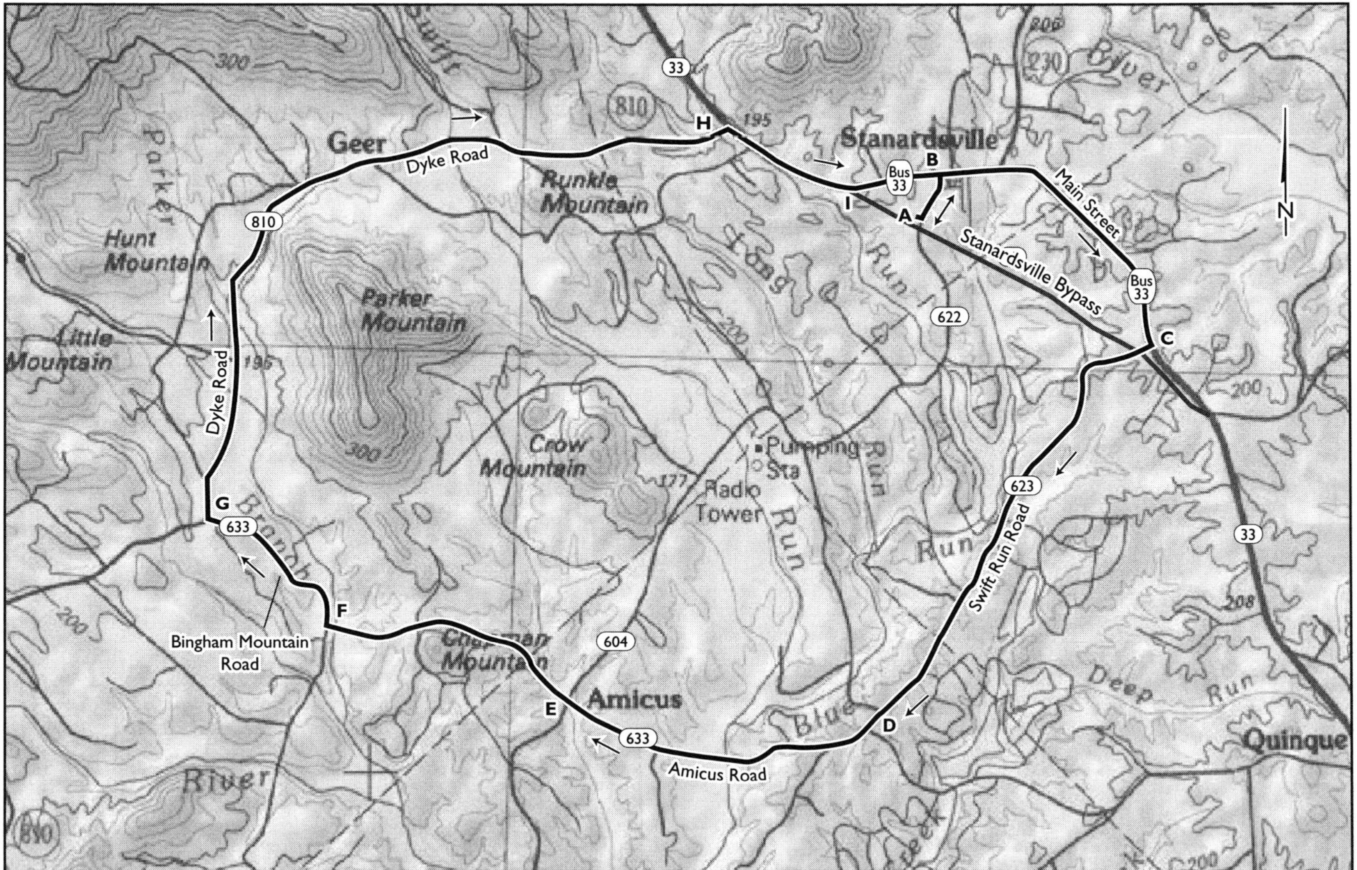
Dyke Road
Geer
Runkle Mountain
Stanardsville
Main Street
Stanardsville Bypass
Hunt Mountain
Parker Mountain
Little Mountain
Crow Mountain
Pumping Sta
Radio Tower
Swift Run Road
Bingham Mountain Road
Chapman Mountain
Amicus
Amicus Road
Quinque
Deep Run
Blue
River
A
B
C
D
E
F
G
H
I
N
33
Bus 33
810
622
623
604
633
230

Ride 45: Stanardsville South

POINT	MILES	DESCRIPTION
A	0.0	Exit William Monroe High School and turn left on Rt 622 Celt Rd
B	0.2	Right on Business Rt 33 Main St, which becomes Spottswood Trail
C	2.1	Cross Rt 33 Stanardsville Bypass. This road becomes Rt 623 Swift Run Rd
D	4.9	Right on Rt 633 Amicus Rd
E	6.8	Cross Rt 604 Celt Rd
F	8.4	Right on Rt 633 Bingham Mtn Rd
G	9.4	Right on Rt 810 Dyke Rd
H	14.0	Right on Rt 33 Spottswood Trail (aka Stanardsville Bypass)
I	14.5	Left to cross median and on to Business Rt 33, which becomes Main St
B	15.4	Right on Rt 622 Celt Rd
A	15.6	Finish at William Monroe High School

Recommended Reading

and Other Resources

Maps (Paper and Software)

The titles below are a great place to start if you want to explore on your own using maps of the locales covered in this book or of other nearby places.

Virginia Atlas and Gazetteer (4th ed) by DeLorme. Rand McNally (2000). ISBN 0-89933-326-5.

Commonwealth of Virginia maps prepared by the Virginia Department of Transportation (1997). Roads correct to July 1, 1995. See the following titles: *Albemarle County, Augusta County, Greene County, Rockingham County.* Supplemental maps covering certain cities and towns within these counties are available.

Back Roads Explorer: TOPO! Maps of All 50 States, software by National Geographic.

TOPO USA, software by DeLorme.

Basic Cycling Information

The titles below will help you with topics like bike maintenance and repair, nutrition, training, and climbing.

Zinn's Cycling Primer: Maintenance Tips and Skill Building for Cyclists by Lennard Zinn. VeloPress (2004). ISBN 1-931382-43-3.

Bicycling Magazine's Complete Book of Road Cycling Skills: Your Guide to Riding Faster, Stronger, Longer, and Safer by Ed Pavelka. Rodale Books (1998). ISBN 0-87596-486-9.

Smart Cycling: Successful Training and Racing for Riders of All Levels by Arnie Baker. Fireside (1997). ISBN 0-684-82243-1.

The Cyclist's Training Bible (3rd ed) by Joe Friel. VeloPress (2003). ISBN 1-931382-21-2.

Zinn and the Art of Road Bike Maintenance by Lennard Zinn, Todd Telander, and Jonathan Vaughters. VeloPress (2000). ISBN 1-884737-70-6.

Zinn and the Art of Mountain Bike Maintenance (4th ed) by Lennard Zinn. VeloPress (2005). ISBN 1-931382-59-X.

Shops and Touring

Need help with your bike? Looking for an organized tour? Try these resources.

Harrisonburg

East Coast Bicycle Academy, 540-433-3013, http://www.emu.edu/students/soa562/index.html

Mark's Bike Shop, 540-434-5151

Shenandoah Bicycle Co., 540-437-9000, http://www.shenandoahbicycle.com

Shenandoah Mountain Touring Co., 540-434-2087, http://www.mtntouring.com

Dayton

Mole Hill Bikes, 540-879-2011, http://www.molehillbikes.com

Staunton

None

Waynesboro

Cycle-Recycle, 540-949-8973, http://cyclerecycle.com

Rockfish Gap Outfitters, 540-943-1461, http://www.rockfishgapoutfitters.com

Charlottesville

Basic Cycles, 434-923-0355, http://www.basiccycles.com

Bike Factory, 434-975-2453, http://www.bikefactory.com

Blue Wheel Bicycles, 434-977-1870, http://www.bluewheel.com

C'ville Bike & Tri, 434-975-1900, http://www.cvillebike.com

Performance Bike Shop, 434-963-9161, http://www.performancebike.com

Other

Adventure Cycling Association (Missoula, MT), 800-755-2453, http://www.adventurecycling.org (Provider of maps for 1976 Bikecentennial route running through central Virginia)

Bike Virginia, 757-229-0507, http://www.bikevirginia.org (Annual host of multiday mass bike tour, often running through the Shenandoah Valley or central Virginia)

Shenandoah Fall Foliage Bike Festival (Staunton), 540-885-26568, http://www.shenandoahbike.org (Festival held annually in the Shenandoah Valley)

Area Cycling Clubs

Harrisonburg

Shenandoah Mountain Bike Club (SMBC), http://shenandoahmountainbikeclub.com/

Shenandoah Valley Bicycle Club (SVBC), http://www.svbikeclub.org/

James Madison University Cycling Team, http://orgs.jmu.edu/cycling/

Waynesboro

Milepost Zero Bicycle Club, http://www.milepostzero.homestead.com/

Charlottesville

Charlottesville Area Mountain Bike Club (CAMBC), http://www.cambc.org/

Charlottesville Bicycle Club (CBC), http://home.earthlink.net/~sgdowell/cbcmain.htm

Charlottesville Racing Club (CRC), http://www.cvilleracing.org/

Charlottesville Triathlon Club (CTC), http://www.cvilletriathlete.com/

University of Virginia Road Cycling Team, http://www.student.virginia.edu/~cycling/

University of Virginia Mountain Bike Club, http://www.student.virginia.edu/~bikeclub/